A GUIDE TO WRITING
SOCIOLOGY PAPERS

The Sociology Writing Group
University of California, Los Angeles

CONSTANCE COINER	NANCY A. MATTHEWS
ARLENE DALLALFAR	JUDITH RICHLIN-KLONSKY
LISA FROHMANN	WILLIAM G. ROY
ROSEANN GIARRUSSO	ELLEN STRENSKI

Coordinators and Editors:
Judith Richlin-Klonsky and Ellen Strenski

ILLUSTRATIONS BY HANNAH BALTER

ST. MARTIN'S PRESS   NEW YORK

Library of Congress Catalog Card Number: 85-61301
Copyright © 1986 by St. Martin's Press, Inc.
All Rights Reserved.
Manufactured in the United States of America.
09876
fedcba
For information, write St. Martin's Press, Inc.
175 Fifth Ave., New York, N.Y. 10010

ISBN: 0-312-35307-3

Cover design: Darby Downey
Cover photograph: Hyungwon Kang and *The Daily Bruin*
Book design: Levavi & Levavi

CONTENTS

TO THE INSTRUCTOR

The quality of student writing is a constant concern to college teachers. Like their colleagues in other disciplines, many sociology instructors, preoccupied by the demands of their profession and dreading the likelihood of poorly written or perhaps plagiarized papers, despair of assigning writing and rely instead on tests. But to do so deprives students of the active, personal engagement with sociological concepts and data that only writing about them can provide. This book is an attempt to do something about this problem.

A Guide to Writing Sociology Papers grew out of our collective experiences as sociology and English faculty members, teaching assistants, counselors, and tutors at UCLA. The book is designed to relieve you of some of the burden of writing instruction and to provide your students—from beginning to advanced—with practical advice. Its format is flexible enough to accommodate specific modifications, yet "spelled out" enough to guide those who need to pay special attention to all steps in the writing process, from initial conceptualization to final presentation.

The underlying premise of the book is that thinking and writing are integrally related—that is, to write a sociology paper is to exercise "the sociological imagination." Our advice and examples are informed throughout by this practical pedagogical observation. For example, when instructors comment to students that their papers are "too psychological" or "really didn't address a sociological issue," students tend to be confused and rarely know how to correct the problem in later papers. Similarly, comments that a paper "has no structure," "follows no clear logic," or "lacks sufficient evidence" often baffle students. Our goal here is to provide both you and your students with illustrations and a common language for discussing and improving papers in these areas.

The book can be used in a variety of ways in both lower- and upper-division sociology courses. It can simply be assigned as a reference for students to consult on their own. You can refer in class or in discussion sections to specific parts when you mention papers, explaining how students can apply our advice to your assignment and how our sample student papers do or do not represent what you expect. Or, in comments on drafts or in individual conferences with students, you can refer students to specific pages in the text.

This book can also be used in a range of writing classes from remedial to advanced. It is especially appropriate for adjunct writing courses paired with sociology courses. However, since much of the advice we present can be generalized to other disciplines, it is also suitable as a basic text in advanced writing courses emphasizing the social sciences. Much of the book—Chapters 2, 3, 5, 6, 7, and Part III—applies equally to the humanities.

While we focus on priorities most commonly identified by instructors, our own writing style is intentionally "student-friendly." Students report that learning about writing is sometimes boring, and for some intimidating. Thus our tone is deliberately easygoing, avoiding prohibitions where possible, including contractions where they soften the prose, and offering guidelines rather than commandments. We also include many specific examples, some taken from student papers, to make the guidelines less abstract.

Acknowledgments

A climate favorable to a project such as ours has been created at the University of California, Los Angeles, by UCLA Writing Programs, the Academic Advancement Program, the Academic Resource Center, and the UCLA reference librarians. We appreciate their continuing support of our common efforts.

Production of the pamphlet on which this book is based was funded by the UCLA Office of Instructional Development. The UCLA Department of Sociology and UCLA Writing Programs provided supplementary clerical support.

We thank Jeffrey Alexander and Melvin Pollner, both of UCLA, for their help in locating appropriate student papers. Special thanks go to the student authors themselves—Ellen Berlfein, Lisa Berry, Sandra Ducoff Garber, and Alvin Hasegawa—for their permission to use their work as examples.

Alice M. Roy, Coordinator of the Writing Program at California State University, Los Angeles, made helpful suggestions on "Logic and Structure" in the first chapter. Several members of the Department of Sociology, UCLA, provided valuable comments on earlier drafts of Part 2: Robert M. Emerson and Linda S. Shaw ("Ethnographic Field Research"); Kenneth Bailey and Gina Randolph ("Quantitative Research"). Professor Emerson also generously granted permission to adapt sections of the guidelines on ethnographic field research he distributes to his students.

Michael Weber, sociology editor in the College Division of St. Martin's Press, recognized the widespread need for a book such as this, and our group is grateful for his support. Charles Briel, St. Martin's sales representative in our area, also deserves our thanks, as does Anne McCoy, project editor for the book. Saul Feinman, of the University of Wyoming, provided an unusually thorough review of the manuscript in which he offered excellent suggestions about the shape it should take.

Above all, this book could not have been conceived or created without the innumerable sociology students whose writing processes we have shared as instructors, tutors, teaching assistants, counselors, and writing consultants. We have been enriched by their efforts to expand their sociological imaginations and to convey their new insights and knowledge in written form.

The Sociology Writing Group

TO THE STUDENT

If you're uneasy about the prospect of writing a sociology paper, you're not alone. Many students feel as you do; that's why we wrote this book. We can't promise that the assignment will be easy, but it *can* be done, and done well. This book can help you feel in control of the writing process from beginning to end, and it can help you produce your best work.

We've written the guide we wish we'd had as undergraduates. We learned too late what "explicate" means. We didn't know how to include our field notes. We had to return to the library at the last minute to find page numbers for passages we needed to cite because we neglected to jot them down in the first place, and we experienced many other problems in writing our own papers. We want to spare you some of the trouble we endured. And we have learned that procrastination—our own and that of others—is not always the result of laziness but often a sign of uncertainty about just how to begin and complete a given writing task.

Our students often tell us that they don't know what they're expected to do in a paper or that they don't know what the instructor wants. So we've tried to demystify the whole process. For example, we explain in Chapter 1 what makes a sociology paper different from papers in other disciplines and what sociology instructors want in terms of a paper's logic and structure. We suggest ways to get started and to stay on track, ways to deal with and present your data, and ways to troubleshoot your writing and to make your prose professional. All along the way our book gives practical illustrations, including some sample student papers you can match with your own. These papers are very good but not perfect. We have commented on their fine features and suggested alternatives where they illustrate problems.

We recommend that everyone read Part I on "Essentials" and Part III on "Finishing Up." Chapters in Part II, on "Writing from Various

Data Sources," can be used selectively. Use the table of contents and the index to look up what you need.

In Part I, Chapter 1 begins with the conceptual starting points which are fundamental for writing a good sociology paper; this chapter also includes the first sample paper by a UCLA undergraduate student. Chapers 2, 3, 4, and 5, respectively, present basic guidelines about organizing your time; writing and revising; keeping track of citations, notes, and references; and avoiding plagiarism. Follow these guidelines from the beginning of your project.

Treat Part II on "Writing from Various Data Sources" as a reference tool. Read the introduction, and then delve into the individual chapters as you need them. These chapters cover four typical kinds of sociology papers that are, in turn, based on four different data sources: the library research paper (Chapter 6), the textual analysis paper (Chapter 7), the ethnographic field research paper (Chapter 8), and the quantitative research paper (Chapter 9). The chapter on library research includes a list of specialized sociological reference sources, and the other three chapters contain three more student papers as illustrations.

Part III on "Finishing Up" is again for everyone. It contains two short but crucial chapters: a checklist to help you polish your final draft (Chapter 10) and guidelines for the last step—typing and submitting your paper (Chapter 11).

Don't sit down and try to read the whole book at one go. Chapter 2 and all the chapters in Part II are meant to guide you through steps in a process. Use these chapters as you would instructions for assembling anything—first scan the chapter to get a sense of what you're in for and then consult it carefully as you move along step by step. Sometimes writing assignments can loom as enormous, mysterious tasks because students don't know how to break them into smaller, more manageable tasks. This guide does that for you. There may be portions of the guide that you'll have to reread before they make sense to you, and other portions that you'll refer to again and again for present and future writing assignments.

The primary purpose of this book is, of course, to help you prepare good sociology papers, and, except for Chapter 9 on quantitative research, which is more technical than the other chapters, you'll be able to use this book from day one of any sociology course. But you'll also find that much of this book applies as well to other social sciences. And many parts will even help you write papers in the humanities. So *A Guide to Writing Sociology Papers* will help you from start to finish of your college career.

Your own campus may offer other resources to help you further.

• Find out if your campus library offers tours so that you can get an overview of its organization. A short time invested at the beginning

of the quarter or semester when schedules tend to be less demanding may save you many hours of wandering and wondering later.
- Find out if your English department offers composition courses in which you can practice these writing skills. Investigate writing courses even after you have fulfilled the common requirement for freshman composition. (Don't let English majors corner the market on intermediate or advanced courses.) At some colleges special writing courses are attached to sociology and other courses, a combination which benefits you doubly. If you are concerned that with your present writing skills you might not get a high grade in a composition class, check out the possibility of taking it as an elective on a pass/no pass basis.
- Find out if your campus has a tutoring center where peer or professional tutors can review your work with you and help you strengthen your skills.

A Note on Our Own Writing Style

Before going on, we would like you to note two features of our own writing: our occasional use of contractions (for example, "we've" instead of "we have") and our avoidance of sexist language.

First, we have tried to make this book as down-to-earth and practical as possible. We imagine ourselves talking to you as we talk to our own students—trying to be direct, friendly, and helpful. Our prose is therefore rather informal and includes contractions. Academic papers, on the other hand, have a different purpose and are usually more formal. Some instructors might object to your using contractions in a sociology paper.

Second, we have deliberately used inclusive language when we refer to people in general. Historically, masculine nouns and pronouns have been used to refer to women and men both—for example, "*Man* is a social animal." As a result of the women's movement, this usage is slowly changing. The checklist in Chapter 10 explains ways of avoiding sexist language.

Finally, we wish we could show you some of our own messy drafts of this book. Writing anything worthwhile—a paper or a book—is always a messy, frustrating, creative, and finally rewarding process. Our own experience has been typical. Final written work usually looks so neat that it's easy to forget the wastepaper baskets overflowing with outlines scribbled on scratch paper, penciled drafts, cut and pasted revisions, and annotated computer printouts. For example, the word processing program on one of our computers automatically counts the number of times a finger touches a key as each document is typed. Writing Chapter 6 involved over 80,000 keystrokes, as we typed in material, rearranged it, changed it, added to it, replaced it, or erased it. So don't be discouraged if you don't like what you first write. That's normal. The paper will improve, and you will like it better with each succeeding keystroke or pencil mark. *A Guide to Writing Sociology Papers* will show you how this happens and will guide you through the process.

PART I

ESSENTIALS

Perhaps the most disabling myth about intellectual activity is that writing is an art that is prompted by inspiration. Some writing can be classified as an art, no doubt, but the art of writing is a trade in the same sense that plumbing or automotive repair are trades. Just as plumbers and mechanics would rarely accomplish anything if they waited for inspiration to impel them to action, so writers would rarely write if they relied on inspiration.

RODNEY STARK,
Sociology

Writing is a craft as well as an art. As with any other craft, becoming a good writer requires understanding the principles of how papers work. A first-rate plumber must know some principles of hydraulics and an outstanding auto mechanic, the principles of combustion. Writing a good sociological paper requires understanding principles of both sociology and writing.

Part I presents these fundamentals of craftsmanship. Chapter 1, "Getting Started," explains some topics that might be considered as much inspiration as perspiration, such as how to use a "sociological imagination" in writing. More specifically, this chapter covers some of the qualities that instructors look for in papers but that students sometimes have difficulty grasping. An instructor will frequently criticize student papers as being "not sufficiently sociological," "not addressing a real question," or "having problems of logic and structure." But often students are not sure what the instructor means, and instructors often find themselves at a loss how exactly to interpret their own comments. So we have explained what sociologists mean when they require papers to "take a sociological perspective," to be "logical and well structured," and to "answer a well-formed question." A sample student paper then illustrates these features.

Starting a paper at all and then staying on a productive schedule is troublesome for many students, so Chapter 2, "Organizing Your Time: The Time Grid," has some practical advice about this problem. Chapter 3, "Writing and Revising," recommends techniques for harnessing the power of the writing process itself to trigger insights and to continually clarify your ideas. Chapter 4, "Citations, Notes, and References," shows how to acknowledge sources of information in your paper, and Chapter 5, "Avoiding Plagiarism," explains how to respect the integrity of these sources when you quote or paraphrase.

Chapter 1

GETTING STARTED

Additionally, and especially in the social sciences, much unclear writing is based on unclear or incomplete thought. It is possible with safety to be technically obscure about something you haven't thought out. It is impossible to be wholly clear on something you do not understand.

JOHN KENNETH GALBRAITH,
"Writing, Typing, and Economics"

Writing a good sociology paper starts with asking a good sociological question. Picking a topic is just the beginning of planning your paper. You need to frame your paper's topic in the form of a *question*. Asking a good question will make the other tasks of writing your paper much easier and will help you hand in a good finished product.

Everything else follows from the question your paper asks. Think of taking a photograph. The deepest artistic sensitivity or the most sophisticated technical skills cannot create a beautiful picture unless you point the camera in the right direction. But carefully aiming the camera in the right direction can combine with simple competence and a personal point of view to produce a fine and, if you are lucky, breathtaking photograph. Likewise, when you create a sociology paper, you can produce interesting, high-quality results without being the smartest or most eloquent student in the world: the key is to take the time to "point" your work in an effective direction by asking a well-formulated question.

Sometimes instructors assign papers by requiring students to respond to a particular question. The sample paper at the end of this chapter was written in response to such an assignment. The student author, Lisa Berry, was asked by her instructor whether a concept covered in the course (the "Cadillac commuter system") helps us understand a particular situation (transportation in the city of Los Angeles). The specific question was "Does Whitt's concept of a Cadillac commuter system apply to Los Angeles?" (Whitt was the theorist who developed this concept of a commuter system serving the elite.)

The question Lisa's instructor posed has no one, short, correct answer. It depends. Just exactly what it depends on is the author's responsibility to state. In some ways the concept applies; in some ways it does not. Deciding where to make the distinctions and arguing for the resulting position is a student's main task in writing a paper.

Even when the assignment is not presented as a question, you must formulate one to address in your paper. Three features distinguish a question that will serve as a strong foundation for a sociology paper. First, a helpful question reflects an understanding of sociology's distinctive perspective on human life. Second, it is carefully posed and framed. Third, it is asked in such a way that it lends itself to a logical and well-structured answer (in contrast to a question that suggests an endless list, such as "What are all the roles adopted by leaders?" or is too open-ended, such as "Why are people irrational?"). The following sections will help you to meet these three criteria for asking good questions.

What Is Sociology?

Failing to understand what sociology is and what sociologists do is a main reason that students experience difficulty in writing successful sociology papers. Since asking a good sociological question depends on understanding what sociology is, this section defines sociology and discusses how it is different from other fields.

Sociology is the study of human social behavior. Its basic insight is that human behavior is shaped by interaction among people. In other words, who a person is, what she or he thinks and does, is affected by the groups of which that person is a member. Sociologists investigate how individuals are shaped by their social groups, from families to nations, and how groups are created and maintained by the individuals who compose them.

Another part of sociology's insight is that interaction takes place in ways which are patterned, even though the people involved may be separated by many years or many miles or may appear to have differences. For example, societies at different historical times or in different geographical locations all find ways to enforce rules, to teach children valued beliefs, and to organize the production of goods necessary to their members' welfare. Sociologists try to understand the consistencies in these processes—the ways in which their similarities and differences follow a predictable pattern.

Sociology and Other Perspectives on Human Behavior

Sometimes new students (and more experienced ones!) are confused about how sociology is distinguished from other disciplines which study people, such as psychology, political science, history, philosophy, anthropology, or economics. In fact, these fields are not totally distinct. Sometimes the interests shared by different fields are easy to see, as with political sociology and political science, for example. But even when the overlap is less apparent, some theorists and researchers in each field share concerns and methods with those in neighboring disciplines.

Right now, however, we want to focus on what is distinctive about sociology because, in order to write successfully in any discipline, you need to have some idea of its boundaries. Our brief sketch necessarily simplifies the definitions of sociology and its "neighbors" and exaggerates their dissimilarities. The differences discussed below are intended primarily to sensitize you to sociology's distinctive features; they are not rigidly observed by theorists or researchers. In fact, many scholars describe themselves explicitly in terms that cross these boundaries (such as social historians, political economists, and social psychologists), often incorporating a sociological perspective into other disciplines.

The following summary compares and contrasts sociology with psychology, political science, history, philosophy, economics, and anthropology. We have illustrated their differences by showing how researchers in each field might approach one aspect of human life—deviant behavior.

Sociology and psychology

Similarities: Both are concerned with attitudes, beliefs, behavior, emotions, and interpersonal relationships.

Differences: Psychology is more likely to focus on the individual level of human behavior. When sociology considers the individual, it is within the context of social groups.

Studying deviance: Psychologists investigate the categories of mental disorders underlying deviant behavior. A sociologist might try to discover whether members of one socioeconomic class are more likely than members of another class to be labeled "mentally ill."

Sociology and political science

Similarities: Both are concerned with government.

Differences: Political scientists analyze different forms of government and their underlying philosophies and study the political process. A sociologist is more likely to examine the interrelationship between political structure and behavior and other aspects of society, such as the economy, religious institutions, and the attitudes of various social groups.

Studying deviance: A political scientist might analyze laws regulating deviance. A sociologist might examine how such laws change as the members of society adopt different ideological beliefs or how they serve the interests of some classes more than others.

Sociology and history

Similarities: Both look at human life over time.

Differences: Historians are more likely to focus on the influence of individuals and on the causes of specific events. Sociologists concentrate on the causes and effects of changes in patterns of social life, among both famous and ordinary people.

Studying deviance: An historian might interpret the motivations and actions of influential deviant individuals and attempt to explain their influence. A sociologist is more likely to trace changes in society's ways of defining and controlling deviant behavior.

Sociology and philosophy

Similarities: Both are interested in beliefs about the nature of life.

Differences: Philosophy is a system of abstract reasoning that follows specific rules of logic. Sociology is empirical: it seeks to discover information about the real world by gathering data about what people actually do.

Studying deviance: Philosophers might ask "What is good?" and "What is evil?" or analyze the appropriate uses of the term "deviance." Sociologists stick to what actually goes on in the social world, asking, for instance, "What do members of this particular society or subculture believe is 'right' and 'wrong'?"

Sociology and anthropology

Similarities: Both are concerned with social life, including culture, beliefs, decision-making, relationships, and so on.

Differences: Anthropology is more likely to study societies other than our own, and to compare aspects of society cross-culturally.

Studying deviance: Anthropologists might travel to an isolated, nonindustrialized society to study how it defines and treats deviant behavior, or might compare differences in rates of deviance in industrialized societies and nonindustrialized societies. Sociologists often study the same processes, but are more likely to focus on a single society.

Sociology and economics

Similarities: Both are concerned with how society produces and distributes goods and services.

Differences: While an economist concentrates on the economy in its own right, sociologists are more likely to consider how the economy affects and is affected by other social processes.

Studying deviance: An economist might study the contributions and costs of deviance to the gross national product. A sociologist might study how the control of the economy by upper social classes provokes deviant behavior, such as burglary and theft, by those without access to a fair share of goods and services.

The Sociological Imagination

One way to describe what is distinctive about a sociological point of view is the "sociological imagination," a phrase coined by C. Wright Mills (1959). Using the sociological imagination means recognizing the connection between individual, private experience and the wider society. Mills calls the personal level an individual's "biography"; he uses the term "history" to refer to patterns and relationships on the larger scale of society. (As you can see, it is sociologists who focus on what Mills calls "history," and historians who concentrate on what he refers to as "biography"!)

As a student, for example, you have followed your own life path to college. Being a college student is part of your personal life story. Your family has its own beliefs about what a college education means. You have your own academic and career goals. You have individual feelings and attitudes about the subjects covered in your classes and your own mixture of college and work schedules. All these things make up your personal, *biographical,* experience of your life as a college student.

Applying sociological imagination to your college life expands your perspective. It is like a wide-angle lens that allows you to see yourself in a larger, more complex (and, in many ways, more interesting) picture. Using sociological imagination, you can begin to see where your experience as a college student fits into the social world in which you live, the *history* of which your biography is a part. Perhaps you are part of a trend among your peer group to major in computer science or communication studies. It could be that you are part of an ethnic group whose members are underrepresented in higher education. Perhaps your academic goals have been affected by social values (say, an increasing emphasis on the need for a college degree), or maybe your career choice, combined with many others', will affect the way society's workforce is balanced between producing goods and providing services.

To use sociological imagination, then, is to identify the intersection of biography and history, the ways in which people are affected by social forces and social groups are affected by their members. As Mills (1959) himself put it,

> Every individual lives, from one generation to the next, in some society; . . . he [or she] lives out a biography, and . . . he lives it out with some historical sequence. By the fact of his living he contributes, however minutely, to the shaping of his society and its history; even as he is made by society and by its historical push and shove. (6)

Mills's deceptively simple insight—that people both affect their own destiny *and* are swept by currents of history—challenges and eludes sociologists from freshmen just starting to study the field to seasoned scholars. The key to using sociological imagination is to not lose sight of either side of this apparent paradox.

Sociology's Focus and Methods

Like other disciplines, sociology has several major subdisciplines— variations on a theme, as it were. Some focus on large-scale "macro" phenomena such as political activities or economic relations. Some focus on "micro" activities which occur on a face-to-face basis such as in families, small groups, or work settings, or among friends. Like- wise, sociology may examine events which are as momentary as the

eye contact between strangers on a bus or as long-term as the indus-
trialization of society. It may deal with social life in terms of its
structure, attempting to uncover stable, underlying patterns, or it
may look at the interactional processes through which individuals
relate socially.

Sociology's methods vary considerably, but all are rooted in science. Basically, this means that sociologists systematically collect
information about the social world and then analyze this verifiable
evidence, or data. The data may come from any of a number of
sources—from controlled laboratory experiments, from written ac-
counts of social life, or from observing, interviewing, or surveying
people involved in the phenomenon being investigated. (In Part II of
this book, we present tips on how you can use four different data
sources, which represent the most typical sources on which undergraduate sociology papers are based.)

From their data, sociologists try to develop theories which explain
what they observe. A theory is an explanation which the theorist
claims can be generalized to all cases of the phenomenon under investigation. A strong theory must be supported by data.

The research process does not end with the proposal of a theory.
Other researchers often use earlier theories to develop questions for
other studies. In some instances they are trying to verify that the
theory is correct—that the general explanation fits their own observations. At other times, they are challenging the validity of the theory
because of differences between what they observe and what the theory
suggests, and they want to offer an alternative explanation.

The question-and-answer process in sociological research follows
one of two general patterns. It may be essentially *deductive* in nature:
asking a question; using previously proposed theories to suggest an
answer (or "hypothesis"); collecting and analyzing data to determine
whether the hypothesis is accurate. Or it may be basically *inductive:*
asking a question; collecting data; using the data to develop a hypothesis in answer to the question. The main difference, obviously, is
whether data are collected in order to test the hypothesis (deductive)
or to create it (inductive).

Sociology not only encompasses a wide range of approaches to research and theory; sociologists also apply those approaches to questions about an innumerable array of topics. In sociology classes you
might study anything from the sociology of sports to the sociology of
religion. You might learn about how those engaged in different occupations perceive their work lives, how a thief accomplishes her or his
crime, or how children learn table manners. You might study birth-
rates, medical decision-making, or the sex lives of teenagers in the
1930s as compared with the 1980s. For each of these subjects, there
are sociologists who disagree about what kinds of questions should be

asked and what methods should be used to answer them. Some sociology departments specialize in one topic or method. But usually they include faculty who represent a range of sociological concerns and styles. Course curricula, including writing assignments, reflect this variety, and students typically have the opportunity to become familiar with several ways of asking and answering sociological questions. When you are trying to understand what an assignment requires of you, it will help to keep in mind the focus of the course as a whole and the particular approach your instructor is presenting.

Sociology, then, is a diverse field. But, across all sociological methods and topics, a sociological perspective involves seeing individuals interacting as members of social groups. As you prepare to formulate the question that will underlie your sociology paper, remember that *adopting the sociological perspective is always the first step* in writing a successful paper.

Framing a Question

Writing a good sociology paper requires using your sociological imagination to frame an interesting question that then guides your research effort. Asking a sociologically imaginative question is one of the tasks students find most challenging and most difficult to pin down. There is no magic recipe, but here are some tips that might help. Your instructor may feel that some aspects of what we say are more important than others, so remember that these are just suggestions.

Remember the "history" part of the sociological imagination. Avoid overly individualistic or psychological questions, questions that concern only what happens inside a person's head. For example, asking whether criminals are motivated more by aggression than by greed is more interesting psychologically than sociologically. (We are in no way implying that psychological questions are inferior to sociological

Framing a Question

questions, but for our purposes here we are emphasizing the sociological aspects of human life.) A sociologically imaginative question might ask what aspects of social life—such as race, class, or gender—influence people to act out their aggression or greed in socially acceptable or unacceptable ways. **Remember the "biography" part of the sociological imagination.** Avoid overly economic questions that drop people out of the picture. (Again, economic questions are often interesting and important, but we want to emphasize the sociological aspects.) For example, asking how much income is lost to crime each year is less sociologically imaginative than asking what types of crime typically victimize wealthy people as compared to poor people.

Ask a question concerning *differences* between individuals, groups, roles, relationships, societies, or time periods. Only rarely do sociologists make claims about all people or all societies. They are typically more interested in how and why people or societies differ from each other; that is, they more frequently ask questions about variation than about uniformity. For example, they would probably not ask whether people are by nature aggressive but rather why some people are more aggressive than others. And are highly aggressive people socialized differently, part of a different subculture, vulnerable to different social pressures, or aspiring to different goals than less aggressive people?

The remaining four suggestions apply to questions for any discipline, not just sociology.

Ask a question that has more than one plausible answer. The paper's task is to demonstrate why your answer is more valid than other plausible answers. You must argue why your answer is more correct and convincing than alternative answers. It wastes both your time and your reader's to belabor the obvious. For example, whether there is widespread public opinion against violent crime can only have one plausible answer. No one would seriously claim otherwise. Before starting the research, specify different plausible answers to your question. Can you imagine anyone seriously taking the other side? If not, you need to reformulate the question.

Unless your assignment specifies otherwise, ask a question that draws relationships between two or more concepts. (Some exceptions are a definition paper, a "feeling" or reaction paper, a story or narrative paper.) Typically, assigned questions concern the relationship between concepts. Are two concepts (for example, deviance and socialization) empirically associated or not? That is, are deviants likely to be socialized differently from nondeviants? Are two concepts (for example, social prestige and deviance) negatively associated, that is, when one is high, the other is low? For example, are people with high prestige less likely to engage in crime than people with low prestige?

Unless specifically instructed, avoid questions that address only one concept, such as "What is deviance?"

Make sure you have access to the information to answer your question. Although some paper assignments do not require any research outside assigned readings and lectures, many do require you to document your points with evidence. For these papers, you must consider when you ask your question whether you can realistically get the necessary documentation. For example, "Has deviance always existed?" is an interesting question with important consequences for sociological theory. But it would be difficult to document adequately whether prehistoric societies had deviance or not. On the other hand, students are sometimes surprised to discover what information does exist and can be tracked down with a little work, so it is best to check with your instructor if you are unsure.

Make sure your question is answerable in the space allowed. This may be the most elusive of our tips and the one students falter on most frequently. Part of the difficulty is that some instructors expect finer detail of documentation or a more fully developed argument than others. Another problem is that students often don't know how much information they will find until they have done their research. Here are two guidelines. First, ask "middle range" questions that are neither grand, monumental, deep truth questions nor minutely exacting, picky detail questions. Second, check out your question with your instructor before you begin your research.

To sum up this section, then, we want to stress that a good paper should not just be *about* some topic (like mental health, race, gender, or occupations). For example, rather than a paper about social mobility, you might frame and address the question "Is there more opportunity for upward mobility in America today than a hundred years ago?" Notice that this question concerns differences between two fairly specific time periods. And it has more than one plausible answer; reasonable people could disagree about whether there is now more opportunity for mobility or less. Framing an answerable but debatable question is a fundamental, and sometimes the most demanding, part of writing a paper.

Logic and Structure

Logic in writing refers to the relationship between the paper's assertions and its evidence. Structure concerns how the parts of the paper fit together. Sentences are the "trees" of the paper; logic and structure are the "forest." According to one faculty survey, structure and logic are among the most important criteria instructors weigh in grading papers.

Logic demands that a good paper go beyond mere assertion ("This statement is true because I say it is"). The answer to your question, which is your thesis, must be supported by evidence and reasoning. One way to accomplish this is to assume that the reader is naive (a Martian, for example) or skeptical. Try to imagine actively what a naive reader might not understand about what you are saying and explain your points to her or him. Try to imagine the kinds of doubts a skeptic might hold and attempt to convince her or him, just like a debater would.

Structure demands that in a good paper not only should each sentence be well written and make sense; it should also be logically connected to the sentences around it, each paragraph to the paragraphs around it, each section to the sections around it, and all of them to the overall theme of the paper. Whether you write sentence by sentence or begin with a general plan and work down to the level of the sentence, by the time you hand the paper in, you should be able to conceptualize the structure of the whole paper in your head (and, if necessary, to explain that structure to the instructor). This means being able to say in one or two sentences what the paper's main thesis is and how you go about arguing that thesis. Imagine your roommate or a friend asking "What's the point of the paper?" and "Why should the reader believe you?" If you can't answer those questions, you still have work to do before turning in the final draft.

The next step after framing your question is constructing a logical defense of your thesis—why your answer is more correct than alternative answers. This defense requires pieces of evidence that support your thesis. The evidence must be logically connected to the thesis so that you can make the statement (either in your head or in the paper) "If the evidence is true, the thesis is true." Many student papers (and some professional papers) falter here, presenting interesting and important evidence in narrative form, or in a controlled study, or sometimes through reasoned reflection, but then drawing a conclusion that is less than warranted by the evidence presented. So be sure to put aside the actual paper and think through the first three items on the checklist presented in Chapter 10: "What is my thesis? Does my thesis remain evident and central throughout the paper? Have I supported my thesis with adequate evidence?"

Finally, the structure of the paper should reflect the logical connection of the evidence to the thesis. It is the writer's job, not the reader's, to draw the connections between evidence and conclusions and to show how the paper logically proceeds. Thus the paper's introduction, transitions, and conclusions are essential, not just incidental parts of the paper. The *introduction* should state the question that is being answered and specify the plan for answering it. As the paper unfolds, provide guideposts for the reader telling where the paper has gone and where it is going. These *transitions* indicate how sentences, paragraphs, and sections logically fit together. Transitions can be accomplished by phrases like "On the other hand" or single words like "Furthermore." (See Chapter 10 for a list of transitions.) Or they can be stated in sentences like "The last section discussed Durkheim's basic presuppositions; this section will show how those presuppositions influenced his theory of religion." A common writing error is the "non sequitur," a Latin phrase for sentences or paragraphs that have no apparent connection. They often result from a connection that is in the writer's mind but which she or he fails to demonstrate to the reader. A *conclusion* should remind readers where they have been and why you think the thesis has been demonstrated. Try to summarize the paper without repeating specific sentences. This is also the appropriate place to reflect upon the larger implications of your thesis—to answer the question "So what?" But it is not appropriate to present new evidence in the conclusion.

Two Formats of Logic and Structure

We suggest here two formats of logic and structure that are common in sociology papers. There are, of course, other formats which may be appropriate for specific assignments. If the paper assignment does not specify an explicit format requirement, it is often helpful to talk over your format ideas with the instructor.

The "Three-Part Essay" Format This type of paper is most commonly structured in terms of a major thesis (which answers a question) and three supporting "points."

There is nothing magical about the number three; it is a convenient number of points for the length and scope of papers typically written for course assignments. Each of the three points should logically support the thesis. You should be able to say "If point A (or B, or C) is true, the thesis is true." More precisely in terms of formal logic, you need to be able to maintain that "if point A (or B, or C) were *not* true, the thesis would probably not be true."

Take as an example the thesis "Over the last hundred years, educational opportunities in America have opened up the American social structure to more upward mobility."

Point A could be: Educational achievement is more closely connected to high-status jobs than it was a hundred years ago.

Point B could be: Education is more equally accessible to all members of the society than were earlier means of determining people's status.

Point C could be: The content of education relates more to job skills than it did a hundred years ago.

The paper itself is structured around an introduction, discussion of point A, discussion of point B, discussion of point C, and conclusion. The introduction presents the question that is being answered, the general thesis, and usually a plan of the body of the paper. Each point is discussed in turn. Each section usually starts with a claim—a statement of its main point. Often the next sentence is an example of this claim, followed by an explanation of how the example illustrates the point. Then you can elaborate on this point, identify its implications, take issue with some aspects, or provide other types of evidence. Finally, you need to tie it back in with your general thesis and with the argument so far.

You will need at least one paragraph for each discussion section, because that's what a paragraph is—a logical section with one main point. You may need more than one paragraph to deal with each main point, especially if the point is complicated or if you are presenting elaborate evidence. If you do, allocate separate paragraphs to each subpoint or aspect. This often happens when you want to analyze a particularly revealing example and explain to what extent it does, but also does *not*, illustrate a point you want to make. In other words, the discussion gives evidence and reasoning for why the point is true; the discussion also explains the logical connection between that point and the general thesis.

The conclusion then summarizes the overall argument and often offers your personal thoughts about the issue you have discussed.

A modified version of the essay format is also appropriate for a paper based on ethnographic research. If that is the kind of paper you're preparing, follow the structure described in this section, replacing the thesis and supporting claims with three major themes, or three points about a single theme, gleaned from your data. See Chapter 8 for details on this modified application.

The "Journal" Format This is the format often found in articles in major academic journals such as the *American Sociological Review* or the *American Journal of Sociology*. Its organization follows the procedural logic of the "hypothesis testing" mode of conducting research, in which you formally test a specific hypothesis through systematic research. The journal format, although usable for projects other than formal hypothesis testing, is best suited to projects that include some sort of systematic data collection and analysis. Its structure follows this order: Introduction (including the literature review and the statement of hypothesis), Methods, Results, and Discussion. (See Chapter 9 on the quantitative research paper for more detail.)

The Introduction specifies the question that is being answered in your paper and your general thesis. In this section, a "review of the literature" summarizes what other people have written about the topic, explaining why it is an important issue to study and what their answers are. This section should also formally state your hypothesis (for example, "A greater proportion of men today hold higher-status jobs than their fathers did a hundred years ago") and justify why you expect it to be true.

The Methods section reports your research procedure, detailing where you got the data, how the variables were measured, and what sort of analysis you conducted on the data. A reader should be able to replicate your study by following the "cookbook" of your methods section.

The Results section reports in literal terms what the study shows. For instance, "30 percent of men a hundred years ago were in higher-status jobs than their fathers, while 29 percent of men today are in higher-status jobs than their fathers," which is virtually no change. (These numbers are made up for this book. They are not true.)

The Discussion section draws the conclusions and reflects upon the result—for example: "The hypothesis must be rejected. The occupational structure has not opened up. The American promise of an equal chance for all is not yet fulfilled."

The essay and journal formats are illustrated by sample student papers in this book. The paper on quantitative research (Chapter 9) follows the journal format. The sample paper at the end of Chapter 1 demonstrates a three-part essay format. The remaining two sample papers—one based on ethnographic field research (Chapter 8) and one demonstrating a textual analysis (Chapter 7)—are modified versions of the essay format. See the relevant chapters for details on organizing your paper.

A Sample Student Paper

The following paper illustrates the principles we have discussed so far. Lisa Berry, an undergraduate sociology major at UCLA, shows how sociological imagination can reveal sociological issues relevant to transportation systems. Many people in urban communities use a freeway system. Even infrequent freeway travelers are affected by the system, whether by smog or by on-ramp traffic that backs up onto surface streets. Thus, while the freeway system is a physical part of society (this is often called "infrastructure"), it also plays a part in our personal lives. Therefore it is an apt topic for sociological scrutiny.

Lisa compares patterns of usage of the Los Angeles freeways and of San Francisco's subway, the Bay Area Rapid Transit (BART) system, by members of various socioeconomic classes. The paper was written for a political sociology course in the fall of 1983, to respond to the assigned question "Does the concept of the 'Cadillac commuter system' (i.e., a system that primarily serves elites), applied to the San Francisco BART system by J. Allen Whitt in *Urban Elites and Mass*

Transportation (1981), apply as well to the Los Angeles transportation system?" The thesis which Lisa offers in answer to this question is that "historically, the Los Angeles plan was a 'Cadillac commuter system,' but it no longer fits the model of such a system" (see the second paragraph of the essay).

Lisa offers evidence about the past and present nature of the Los Angeles transportation system to support her thesis. For the most part, the logic and structure of her argument are strong. In the commentary accompanying the essay, we have pointed to its strengths and suggested ways to make it even better.

This paper uses the three-part essay format discussed above; our notes on the pages facing the essay signal the main points Lisa makes so that you can see this format in practice. To see a sample paper that uses the journal format, turn to the quantitative paper at the end of Chapter 9.

Our Comments

The title reflects the topic (mass transportation in L.A.) and also the student's thesis (L.A. no longer has a Cadillac commuter system).

This introduction establishes a context for the ideas in the paper so that the reader knows what to expect—not deviance or mobility, but mass transportation. Lisa begins by identifying Whitt's original question and his thesis. She then acknowledges her initial response as she sorted out the data, working toward her own thesis, which she introduces in general form at the end of this first paragraph.

Lisa sets up the problem using the sociological concepts discussed in class—comparing the relationship between the ecological system and class structure of two modern cities.

If Lisa were to revise this paper, we would encourage her not to minimize this "one respect." Proximity to a freeway does not mean much without a means of transportation.

The second paragraph narrows down and focuses the discussion on Lisa's own argument. The original question could be answered in many ways. Lisa must decide which distinctions make sense to her. This position is her thesis. She now specifies her plan for answering the question and previews the paper's structure. She ends this introduction with a clear statement of her thesis, identifying precisely where she stands. In such a short paper, however, her thesis really should have come earlier.

In this paragraph, Lisa begins her first main point, using history to support her argument. She gives concrete examples, followed by more examples and explanations. Notice how the writing flows back and forth between generalizations and specific details that support and explain those generalizations.

Lisa Berry
Sociology 140
Professor Roy
Nov. 23, 1983

L.A.'s Non-Cadillac System

Compton. Santa Monica. Topanga Canyon. Three very
diverse areas—environmentally, economically, and racially—yet
all share a common bond in their need for transportation to
and from downtown Los Angeles. Many of the suburbs house
workers who commute to the central city area daily. Urban
Elites and Mass Transportation by J. Allen Whitt addresses
the issue of mass transportation, asking who develops such
systems and whom the system serves. From his analysis of the
San Francisco transit line, Whitt claims that the BART system
benefits the affluent fraction of the urban population who
work in the downtown San Francisco area (Whitt, 1981). In
comparing the Los Angeles freeway system to the BART system,
I had the feeling of trying to compare apples to oranges. The
two plans provide different forms of transportation, but more
important, the cities are drastically dissimilar in
structure—Los Angeles one of the most dispersed and San
Francisco one of the most highly concentrated cities in the
United States.

After carefully analyzing the layout of the Los Angeles
freeway system, I agree that Los Angeles is a "Cadillac
commuter system," but only in one respect—it serves the
needs of the elite insofar as they have greater means of
transportation (cars) than those in the lower-class suburbs.
Notwithstanding this, it differs from the BART system in that
very few highways pass through the upper-class suburbs en
route to downtown Los Angeles. After studying the development
of the Los Angeles system, I will attempt to prove that
historically the Los Angeles plan was a "Cadillac commuter
system," but it no longer fits the model of such a system.

The Los Angeles transit plan was first developed as a
rail system (Brodsly, 1981). Pacific Electric, Los Angeles'
interurban railway, was the largest of its kind in the world
and greatly shaped the face of the Los Angeles region. For
instance, in 1900, Long Beach had a population of 200.

Notice how Lisa acknowledges the sources of her borrowed information.

This last sentence summarizes this long paragraph, reminding the reader of the main point and preparing the transition to the next point.

Here Lisa introduces her second main point, qualifying the discussion so far. She uses an appropriate transition ("Yet") to signal the contrast.

Again, she gives concrete examples, introducing them with appropriate transitional expressions.

Here Lisa is building evidence from a commonly used archival data source.

"Affluent" is a good application of a sociological concept.

However, when the railway was expanded to include this
suburb, the population burgeoned to a high of 1,700 in less
than ten years (Brodsly, 1981:68). By 1915, Los Angeles had
the largest ratio of cars to people in the world, which led
to tremendous traffic congestion. A traffic commission was
soon developed in hopes of remedying the problem.
Unfortunately, the Great Depression was the demise of an
improved rail system (McWilliams, 1973). Buses and cars
encroached on the trolleys' territory, and rail lines were
transformed into freeways. As freeways began to evolve, a
distinct pattern developed whereby these thoroughfares all
intersected in downtown Los Angeles (obviously at the behest
of the affluent suburbanites and downtown businesses). The
earliest freeways included the Pasadena, Santa Ana, Santa
Monica, and the Hollywood freeways, which not surprisingly
surrounded such posh areas of the early 1900s as Pasadena,
Exposition Park, and Hollywood. Thus, from a historical
perspective, the Los Angeles freeway system developed to
serve the needs of the affluent community to reach the
downtown area.

Yet, by 1950, Los Angeles had experienced drastic
population shifts such that the affluent migrated to the
coastal regions and the poor and racial minorities were
largely forced into the suburbs circumscribing the downtown
region. Once posh areas such as Exposition Park and Pasadena
were now generally inhabited by lower-class or unemployed
black and Hispanic groups. The 1970 census confirms this
population shift. For example, areas such as Compton,
Inglewood, and South Pasadena have populations consisting of
60 to 90 percent blacks. Yet most areas to the west and
northwest—Santa Monica, Beverly Hills, Encino—have a black
population of well under 5 percent (U.S. Bureau of the
Census, 1971). Home values have also shifted. Around
Exposition Park and Pasadena, homes ranged from $18,000 to
$30,000, whereas in Beverly Hills, Bel Air, and parts of
Santa Monica, home values started at well over $50,000.
Although these census figures are outdated, the trend has
persisted.

Today, of the many highways connecting the suburbs to
downtown, only one passes through affluent areas of Los
Angeles, this being the Santa Monica Freeway. Many would

This paragraph expands one aspect of the second main point in the previous paragraph. Lisa considers alternative explanations of the evidence and argues for her own as the best.

In the paper, Lisa uses "elite," "upper class," and "affluent" interchangeably. But sociologists do distinguish special meanings among them, and so should Lisa's paper.

Here Lisa brings in her third point. She relates it to her original position by showing evidence which contradicts Whitt's thesis, again giving examples.

This last paragraph is the paper's conclusion. It reminds the reader of Lisa's thesis, which responds to the original question. It ties together the three main points she made earlier without repeating specific sentences.

argue that the absence of freeways in affluent areas was
intentional. They feel that such thoroughfares increase the
noise level and lower the values of homes in the area.
Although both are valid points, other factors such as the
relative newness of these areas and the general trend toward
less freeway construction must also be taken into account.
Although the upper class still has greater means of
transportation to and from downtown Los Angeles, the system
is no longer exclusively serving the privileged fraction of
the population. In my opinion, when it takes the wealthy
Palos Verdes lawyer or Pacific Palisades stockbroker over
twenty minutes to reach the nearest expressway en route to
downtown Los Angeles, these elites no longer have what Whitt
termed a "Cadillac commuter system."

A more important finding than the circuitous freeway
system of the affluent is the frequency with which the
freeway systems pass through the lower income areas of Los
Angeles. Both these findings contradict Whitt's theory of the
BART transit system. For example, the Pomona Freeway passes
through east Los Angeles, South El Monte, and Hacienda
Heights; the Santa Ana Freeway runs through Downey, Pico
Rivera, and Bell Gardens; and the San Bernardino connects
Alhambra, Rosemead, and El Monte to the downtown area.
Although the lower-class sector's means of transportation are
circumscribed by poverty, they are no longer excluded from
the city's freeway system. In fact, most of the thoroughfares
are situated to serve the needs of the indigent more
efficiently than the affluent sectors of the population.

Clearly, the Los Angeles freeway system is quite
different from San Francisco's BART system. Whereas BART runs
through the affluent areas, bypassing the ghettos, Los
Angeles' freeways run through the lower-class areas and
bypass the affluent sections of the city. This shift signals
a change away from the "Cadillac commuter system" first
identified by Whitt. The affluent originally built the
freeway system to serve their needs in traveling to and from
downtown. Yet, by the 1950s, the elites were beginning to
move west and northwest away from their means of
transportation to the central city area. Within the last few
decades, the transit system has become much more equitable.
Although the affluent have greater means of transportation to

the downtown area, the lower-class sectors have greater
access to the system because of their greater proximity to
it, producing a slow death for the "Cadillac commuter
system" in Los Angeles.

REFERENCES

Brodsly, David
  1981   L.A. Freeway: An Appreciative Essay. Berkeley:
         University of California Press.
McWilliams, Carey
  1973   Southern California: Island on the Land. Santa
         Barbara: Peregrine Smith.
U.S. Bureau of the Census
  1971   1970 Census of Population and Housing: Census Tracts.
         Washington, D.C.: Government Printing Office.
Whitt, J. Allen
  1981   Urban Elites and Mass Transportation. Princeton:
         Princeton University Press.

Here Lisa gives complete bibliographic information about the sources from which she borrowed information.

Chapter 2

ORGANIZING YOUR TIME: THE TIME GRID

It's worth repeating: half the battle is won when the first word is written. You wouldn't believe the wild contortions professional writers go through to avoid writing that first word of the day. Pencils must be sharpened; typewriters cleaned and ribbons changed; filing demands to be done; the cat must be let out; that filthy window must be cleaned; shelves of books must be rearranged; a letter must be mailed; the cat must be let back in.

GENE OLSON,
Sweet Agony: A Writing Manual of Sorts

Here is a tool to get you started—a semester/quarter time grid (see Figure 2-1). The first stage of the writing process can be agonizing for many people. We believe that the key to writing better papers, with less anxiety, is starting early enough to write more than one draft. Many students experience "writer's block" because they think they should be able to produce a finished product on the first try. Paper writing, therefore, seems nearly impossible and is put off until the night before the due date. Then, because writing done at the last minute is often inadequate, the students' doubts about themselves as writers are confirmed. Some students move in a vicious cycle of anxiety, procrastination, and, almost inevitably, disappointing results. A time grid can help you break this pattern and feel more in control of the writing process.

By looking at the whole semester or quarter, you can set up a realistic plan for completing your paper, taking into consideration your exams, other assignments, and other commitments. (We suggest making an enlarged photocopy or hand-drawn version of this time grid so that you can write on it more easily and reuse it every semester or quarter.) Filling in the time grid will pay the following dividends: it forces you to break up what may loom as an enormous task—writing a whole paper in one sitting—into smaller, "do-able" tasks. When you set a beginning date for each small task, you will probably get started sooner and avoid the guilt and anxiety that often accompany procrastination. Moreover, this approach to writing usually results in your learning more and earning a higher grade because you have allowed time for all the steps in the process of preparing a good paper.

Some papers are assigned early in the semester or quarter and are not due until the end, while others are assigned only a few weeks before the due date. Although the time grid is most helpful when you have most of the semester to complete your paper, our advice on organizing your time applies to short-term papers as well. Even when you have only a few weeks to complete your paper assignment, planning will pay off. Planning involves two steps: first, determining your specific writing tasks; and, second, appropriately allocating your time among these tasks.

To set up a work schedule, you must first determine your tasks. For illustration we will use the four most typical kinds of papers assigned in sociology classes: library research, textual analysis, ethnographic field research, and quantitative research. These kinds of papers are discussed in Part II.

The first task for all types of papers is choosing a topic, unless, of course, a topic is assigned. Select a provisional topic as early as possible, because it will probably evolve as you find references and become more familiar with the readings or the field setting. You can never know if a possible topic for a library or quantitative paper will work out until you at least skim some possible sources. Nor can you decide on a topic for an ethnographic field research paper until you get permission to visit the setting and observe the people there.

If you have the whole responsibility for choosing an appropriate topic, consider the guidelines presented in Chapter 1 and this advice from Ellen Berlfein, student author of the sample paper in Chapter 7: "If possible," she recommends, "choose a topic you are interested in, something you have a personal commitment to." She also encourages you to "talk about your topic with others to help formulate your ideas."

Except for topic selection, the four types of papers involve different tasks and therefore different ways of setting up a work schedule. As you can see from Table 2-1, each type of paper requires a different set of tasks to be completed in a certain order. Study this table carefully. As you can see, the beginning and concluding stages of all papers are the same; they all involve selecting a topic, framing an appropriate question, and writing drafts, ideally three drafts (two rough and a final one to turn in). However, each paper has different middle steps: a quantitative paper has seven different middle tasks; an ethno-

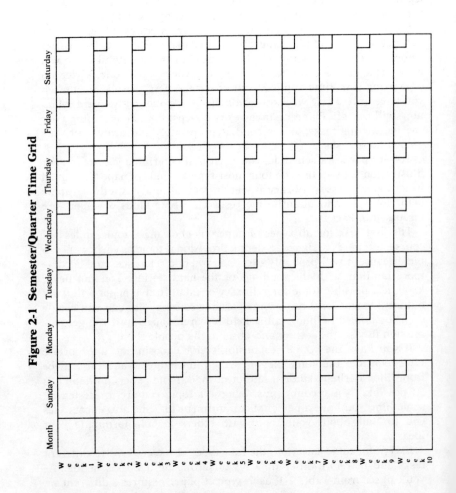

Figure 2-1 Semester/Quarter Time Grid

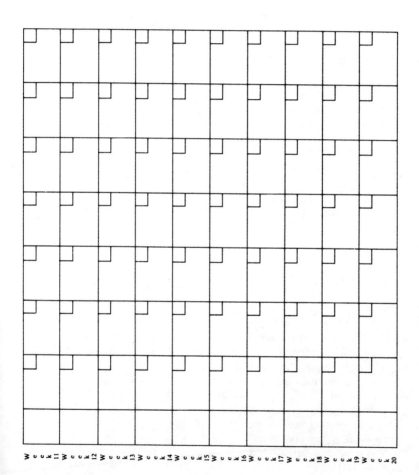

Table 2-1 Determining Your Tasks

	Library	Textual	Ethno-graphic Field	Quanti-tative
Pick and narrow down your topic; frame an appropriate question; verify with your instructor	X	X	X	X
Different middle steps:				
Locate references in the library	X		—[a]	X
Take notes on library references	X		—[a]	X
Take notes for analysis of text(s)		X		
Write a provisional thesis and outline; consult your instructor	X	X		X
Write a plan for data collection and analysis; consult instructor			X	X
Construct data collection instruments, design methods, etc.				X
Collect data			X	X
Analyze data			X	X
Write a rough draft; type draft 1 (and print out, if applicable)	X	X	X	X
Revise; then type draft 2 (and print out, if applicable)	X	X	X	X
Revise, partly by going over the "Checklist for Polishing" (Chapter 10)	X	X	X	X
Read "Guidelines for Typing and Submitting Your Paper" (Chapter 11); type final copy (and print out, if applicable)	X	X	X	X
Proofread, correct, and photocopy	X	X	X	X

[a] These steps are not required of all ethnographic field research papers. You should check with your instructor to determine whether your assignment requires these two steps.

graphic field research paper has five; a library research paper has three; a textual analysis has only two. The way you allocate your time, then, depends on the type of paper you are writing. Your paper schedule will also vary according to the length of your semester or quarter and the time between assignment and due date. Therefore, we can suggest only *general guidelines* for scheduling your time. Once you have selected your topic, we estimate that you should spend approximately 50–70 percent of your time completing the middle steps required for your type of paper. The remaining 30–50 percent of your time should be spent completing the last five steps— from writing your first rough draft to photocopying your final draft— with the majority of that time spent on revising. In Table 2-2 we estimate, for each type of paper, how you should allocate your time among the required tasks.

On the basis of Table 2-2, we can compare and contrast the allocation of time for each type of paper (assuming that the level of difficulty and time allowed for writing do not vary significantly). For a library paper, you will spend much of your time gathering references and taking notes on them. For a textual analysis, you will also spend much of your time reading and taking notes, but you will concentrate on only one or two texts. When you write an ethnographic field research paper, you will spend less time reading references and more time collecting data and recording notes. A quantitative paper requires a combination of tasks. You will devote about a third of your time to library research, another third to designing your study and collecting and analyzing your data, and only the last third to writing your paper. (This description of tasks is simplified; for necessary details about each type of paper see the appropriate chapter in Part II.)

Table 2-2 Allocating Your Time

	Library	Textual	Field	Quantitative
Select topic and references	20%	10%	10%	10%
Read and take notes (including the writing of a provisional thesis, outline, and method plan, if applicable)	30	40	10	30
Collect and analyze data (including the construction of data collection instruments, if applicable)			50	30
Writing, revising, and polishing	50	50	30	30
Total time	100	100	100	100

Now you are ready to work with the time grid. Begin by filling in the name of the month in the first column and the dates in the small boxes (inside the larger boxes). If the month changes in the middle of the week, do not skip down to the next row. Just continue the dates for the new month in the very next box, and go back and label the new month in the first column.

The time grid is long enough to accommodate a 20-week semester. If you are on a shorter semester (15–18 weeks) or quarter system (10 weeks), simply cross out the weeks your college is not in session. Once all the dates are filled in, write in the exams, quizzes, and major assignments from all your classes in the larger boxes corresponding to their due dates. Include any other important deadlines or events that may influence your writing schedule, whether school related or not.

Next, choose a date on the time grid when you will begin each required task listed in Table 2-1 for your type of paper. Write the task in pencil in the large box corresponding to that date. So as not to clutter up the grid, make the beginning dates of new tasks also represent completion deadlines for the previous task. Apportion your time according to Table 2-2. For example, if you are on the quarter system, and at the beginning of the quarter your instructor assigns a quantitative paper to be due at the end of the quarter, you will have a maximum of 9–10 weeks to complete your paper after selecting a topic. Therefore, on your time grid you will divide the first 5–6 weeks of the quarter into days for completing the middle steps of the writing process, and the last 3–4 weeks into days for writing, revising, and polishing your paper. (Figure 2-2 gives a sample time grid for a quantitative paper written during a ten-week quarter.) No matter what type of paper you are writing or how much time you have from assignment to

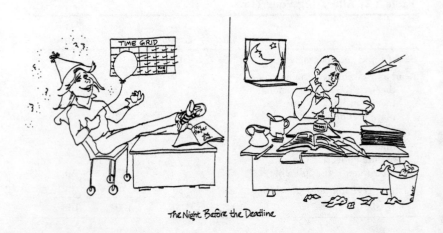

The Night Before the Deadline

due date, be sure to mark off enough time on your time grid to write and/or revise more than one draft. It is also advisable to build your schedule so that it ends *before* the absolute deadline, since unexpected events may keep you from meeting the due date.

As soon as you have selected a topic and framed your question, discuss it with your instructor. Soon afterward show him or her a written thesis, outline, and/or plan for data collection and analysis (if applicable). Thirty minutes with your instructor will lessen anxiety during the remainder of the writing process, which is not a bad trade-off. (You are more likely to get thirty uninterrupted minutes with your instructor if you make an appointment rather than pop in during office hours.)

The semester/quarter time grid will work only if you stick to it. Put it in a prominent place (e.g., taped to a mirror or refrigerator) so you will see it every day. Many students find that the time grid not only helps them produce better papers but also keeps them on top of their other assignments.

38   ESSENTIALS

Figure 2-2 Sample Time Grid for a Quantitative

Month	Sunday	Monday	Tuesday

Week 1 — Oct.
- Sunday 3
- Monday 4
- Tuesday 5

Make an appointment with your instructor.

Week 2
- Sunday 10: Pick & Narrow Down Topic & Frame question
- Monday 11: Verify Topic & Question w. Professor; Locate References
- Tuesday 12: MATH QUIZ

Week 3
- Sunday 17: Start Reading & Note taking
- Monday 18
- Tuesday 19

Week 4
- Sunday 24
- Monday 25: Write Provisional thesis, outline & methods plan; verify with Prof.
- Tuesday 26: MATH QUIZ

Although the month changed, stay on the same line of the time grid. Mark the new month in the first column.

Week 5 — Nov.
- Sunday 31
- Monday 1
- Tuesday 2

Week 6
- Sunday 7: Begin Data Analysis
- Monday 8
- Tuesday 9: MATH QUIZ

Begin your writing early to allow time for revising.

Week 7
- Sunday 14: Begin Writing 1st Rough Draft
- Monday 15
- Tuesday 16

Week 8
- Sunday 21
- Monday 22
- Tuesday 23: MATH QUIZ

Revise partly by going over the "Checklist for Polishing," Chapter 10.

Week 9 — Dec.
- Sunday 28: Begin Revisions of Draft 2 (checklist for Polishing)
- Monday 29
- Tuesday 30

Week 10
- Sunday 5
- Monday 6
- Tuesday 7: MATH QUIZ; proofread, correct, & photocopy

Allow time for proofreading, correcting, and photocopying your paper.

* We have used the quantitative paper for our sample time grid because it has the most steps. Your time grid may have fewer boxes filled in than the one above.

Paper Written During a 10-Week Quarter*

Wednesday	Thursday	Friday	Saturday
6	7	8	9
		Financial Aid Application Due	
13	14	15	16
20	21	22	23
			FOOTBALL GAME AT STATE
Begin 27 Construction of Questionnaires	28	29	Begin 30 Data Collection
3	4	5	6
Psychology EXAM		HISTORY EXAM	
10	11	12	13
	Sociology EXAM		ROCK CONCERT
Type 17 & Print out Draft 1	18	19	Begin 20 Revisions of Draft 1 (resulting in Draft 2)
24	Type & 25 print out Draft 2	History 26 Homework DUE	27
1	2	3	Type 4 & print out final Copy
8	turn in 9 Sociology paper!	10	11

Include other important deadlines or events which may influence your writing schedule.

Allow enough time for data collection and analysis.

Set a date when you will begin each new task. The beginning of a new task signals the completion of the previous task.

Include important due dates for other classes.

It is a good idea to set your paper aside for a few days before revising.

Plan to finish before the due date for self-assurance.

Revise from a typed copy of your draft.

Chapter 3

WRITING AND REVISING

INTERVIEWER: *How much rewriting do you do?*

HEMINGWAY: *It depends. I rewrote the ending of* Farewell to Arms, *the last page of it, thirty-nine times before I was satisfied.*

INTERVIEWER: *Was there some technical problem there? What was it that had stumped you?*

HEMINGWAY: *Getting the words right.*

GEORGE PLIMPTON,
Writers at Work: The "Paris Review" Interviews

Very few writers, including not only students but instructors and professional writers as well, produce presentable material on the first try. Studies have shown that the *very act of writing* triggers insights, helps clarify ideas, and reveals relationships among ideas. Writing is part of the thinking process. Therefore, don't expect your first draft to be presentable. It may have incomplete ideas or even incomplete sentences. The important thing is to begin—often the most difficult part of writing—and put your thoughts, however scrambled, on paper. Once you have some ideas on paper, you can revise, which will improve your paper tremendously. Ellen Berlfein, a student whose paper appears at the end of Chapter 7, says, "I have trouble getting started. I found that if you just start writing, no matter what it sounds like, and get ideas down on paper, then you have something to work with. You can formulate the structure of your paper from these ideas."

Revising includes inserting new ideas and deleting or modifying old ones; rewriting sentences or paragraphs to improve clarity or logic; moving sentences or paragraphs around to strengthen organization; and adding transitions to enhance the flow of your paper and accentuate the relationships among your ideas. Revising can greatly improve the logic and structure of your argument, features of your paper explained in Chapter 1. Toward the end of the writing process, edit your paper by paying attention to mechanical matters such as punctuation and spelling. Setting your drafts aside for a few days between revisions helps you see their strengths and weaknesses more clearly.

We also recommend outlining, in which you identify main ideas and put them down on paper in some order. It forces you to think through the material actively. But at what point in the writing process outlining is undertaken, and with how much detail, varies with assignments and with writers' preferences. Sometimes outlining seems so great a task ("How can I know what I'm going to say before I've said it?") that it becomes an obstacle, not a guide, to writing.

Student Alvin Hasegawa (see his paper in Chapter 9) recommends outlining before the first rough draft: "The only advice I can give to another student is to start writing the paper with an outline. An outline guides the direction of the paper, it lets you get down something concrete to work with, and it gives you an idea of what you have to do." However, we've said that the very act of writing triggers thought, so you may find that outlining comes more easily after you've written some ideas or after your first rough draft. Outlining may take time that you feel should be spent writing the paper, but you will save time in the long run. It's much easier to revise an outline (add, omit, or shift main points) than to repair a completed essay. Moreover, an outline provides you with something concrete to show your instructor long before the paper's due date, to make sure you're on target.

Since revision can best be conducted from typed copies of your drafts, typing also aids your writing. You should type at least one draft before typing the copy you turn in, since problems such as lack of organization and clarity are more apparent in a typed draft. As one writing expert put it:

> The typewriter distances prose and it does it quickly. By depersonalizing our priceless prose, a typescript shows it to us as seen through a stranger's eyes. It tells us what it looks like, literally how it "shapes up." No single bad writing habit is so powerful as the habit of typing an essay only when you are ready to turn it in. Correct the handwritten manuscript by all means, but then type a draft and revise that. . . . The typed draft represents the central mechanical stage in the creative oscillation we go through, that back-and-forth movement in which first we suggest things to the prose and then it suggests things to us. (Lanham, 1979:54)

With a typed copy of your draft you can more easily use the "cut and paste" method of revision, which involves typing a rough draft and then cutting it up and putting it back together in a more logical order, leaving out sentences or paragraphs, or adding new ones. But we caution you to cut up a photocopy of the typed draft rather than the original, since you will probably want to refer to the original.

For the reasons given above, writers who lack typing skill are at a disadvantage, not only in college but also in many jobs. If you cannot type at least moderately well, perhaps you should investigate typing classes in your community; and, although you have little choice but longhand for the writing process, arrange well in advance of the due date to have the final draft typed by a skilled typist. Too many typographical errors (typos) blemish even an otherwise excellent paper.

Typing and revising are easier on a word processor or personal computer. With a computer you can quickly correct typos, move sentences and paragraphs around, and easily produce typed copies of your various drafts. We caution you to carefully proofread your final copy so that it doesn't contain words or phrases from former drafts you meant to delete.

Sandra Ducoff Garber, a student whose paper appears in Chapter 8, enthusiastically recommends word processing: "Using a computer was an immense help. The computer facilitated my style. Its editing capabilities were liberating. Because editing was easier than it would have been with a typewriter, I was more willing to edit the paper over and over again." Learning word processing is not difficult or excessively time-consuming, even for those who have had no prior experience with computers. You can also use word processing skills to write papers for other courses and, perhaps, in a future (or even current) job. Increasingly, colleges are establishing centers on campus where you can arrange to use a computer for course assignments. Find out whether your college has such a center.

We are not recommending that you *compose* your drafts in any particular way. Writing habits vary—some writers prefer to compose in longhand, others at a typewriter, and still others at a word processor. However, to repeat, we strongly recommend revising from a typed copy. (Be sure to print out the copy if you have typed your paper on a computer.) If you compose rough drafts in longhand, next type them, double-spacing and leaving ample margins (don't worry about typing perfectly, since these copies don't go to the instructor). Then revise. The revisions you make right on the typed copy should probably be in pencil, so you can erase if necessary. The limited area on the draft available for revising (margins and spaces between lines) gets depleted quickly if most of it gets blotched from ink that has been scribbled over; your revised draft might become illegible, difficult to work with and to retype. (Long insertions, which require another piece of paper anyway, can be written in ink.)

When revising, think carefully about your paper's key concepts and terms. Define them as you introduce them (usually in the opening paragraphs) and use them accurately throughout the paper. Be especially cautious when using terms originated by sociologists that have become part of everyday language and yet retain special sociological meanings (e.g., "stereotype," "status," "self-fulfilling prophecy"). For example, one of our sample student papers (in Chapter 1) uses terms— "elite," "upper class," and "affluent"—that are synonyms in ordinary language but have separate meanings in sociology. It's often helpful to write out sociological definitions of your central terms on scratch paper—in language you can understand—in order to foster clear and accurate use of them as you revise.

Finally, it's a good idea to locate a manual of style—which presents standards and examples of grammar, punctuation, usage, and typography—to answer specific questions that may arise during the writing process. If your paper includes tables and graphs, choose a manual that also provides guidelines on how such information should be arranged and labeled. (Both style manuals we recommend below include such guidelines and are available in many libraries and bookstores.) Early in the quarter/semester, before the almost inevitable end-of-the-term crunch, ask your instructor to recommend a manual; you can put it aside until you need it. If your instructor doesn't have a preference, we suggest *The Chicago Manual of Style*. However, since this comprehensive manual is currently available only in hardcover, at what may be a prohibitively expensive price, we also recommend the inexpensive, popular paperback edition of Kate L. Turabian's *A Manual for Writers of Term Papers, Dissertations, and Theses*, which recommends many of the same style standards suggested by *The Chicago Manual of Style*. If anxiety about standards and rules impedes your writing, don't even think about the manual until you have generated at least one draft.

Chapter 4

CITATION, NOTES, AND REFERENCES

Pray be precise as to details.

SHERLOCK HOLMES IN CONAN DOYLE'S
"Adventure of the Speckled Band"

Formats for indicating the sources of quotations and borrowed ideas used in written work vary among different sociological books and journals. Your instructor may require a specific format or recommend a particular style manual. If not, the following guidelines follow one citation format widely used in sociology, illustrated in the *American Sociological Review*. In this system:

1. Author and page citations for the quotations or borrowed ideas you use are incorporated into the text of your paper.
2. Comments or additional information are included in "Notes" following the text of your paper, although such "Notes" are rarely used in undergraduate writing.
3. The full publication information for all cited materials is listed in a section at the very end, entitled either "References" or "Bibliography."

Citations in the Text

Authors' names used in the text are followed by the publication date and page number in parentheses.

Example: Matza (1969:3) states that he is presenting "a revised idea of naturalism."

The format is the same if you are paraphrasing, not quoting.

Example: Matza (1969:3) distinguishes his definition of naturalism from definitions used in the past.

When you write a textual analysis (described in Chapter 7), you might use only one source—the book or essay which you are analyzing. In this case, you need to give the publication date only the first time the author's name is mentioned.

Example (first mention of author): Durkheim (1951) claims that suicide is not only an individual event but also a social phenomenon.
    (After first mention) Durkheim describes the role of social factors in suicide.

Note that the page numbers of quotations or of specific claims or evidence should be indicated even after the first mention of the author.

Example: Durkheim (44) defines suicide in a way that leaves all animal deaths out of his study.

Full publication information on the text you use for your analysis should be included in your References or Bibliography (discussed later in this chapter).

At times you may want to cite several authors who discuss a single idea. Then you will have a series of citations which should all be enclosed within parentheses. List authors chronologically (the earliest publication date goes first) and separate the works with semicolons.

Example: Some sociologists question the value of using official statistics in conducting research (Kitsuse and Cicourel, 1963; Cicourel, 1964; Matza, 1969).

For dual authorship, give both last names; for more than two authors, use the first author's name followed by "et al." (but include all the authors' names in the References or Bibliography at the end of the paper).

Example: Many sociologists believe it is important to examine the work of the professionals who claim to treat the physical and mental health of a society (Yarrow et al., 1955; Conrad and Schneider, 1980).

For authors with more than one publication in the same year, designate each work by "a," "b," etc.

Example: Norbert Elias' *What Is Sociology?*, listed below under "Examples of Listings for Books," would be cited in the text as (Elias, 1978b).

If your quotation is longer than five lines, indent all lines five spaces from the left margin (leave the right margin as it is throughout the text) and single space. Quotation marks are unnecessary, since the indented left margin tells your reader that the material is quoted. The quotation from Durkheim, discussed in the following chapter, "Avoiding Plagiarism," is an example of a long quotation.

In rare cases, you may also use this quotation format when you want to emphasize especially important or interesting quoted material. For example, in the sample ethnographic paper the author uses the indented format to highlight quotations that are particularly dramatic but less than five lines long.

Notes

In some disciplines, footnotes (at the bottom of the page) or end notes (following the text) contain the author and page citations which, in sociology, are incorporated into the text. In sociology, however, information which may be of interest to the reader but not directly relevant to the point of the paper may be included in a Notes section following the text. Although this practice is common among professional sociologists, it is rarely necessary in undergraduate writing. Avoid using notes as a way out of organizing your paper by making them a "dump" for materials you are not sure how to integrate. Add notes sparingly, only to express a tangential comment which you feel you *must* make.

References and Bibliographies

The Notes are followed by a list of the source materials you used in writing your paper. Some instructors prefer that you list all materials you consulted in developing your paper, whether or not they are directly incorporated into your paper; in this case the list is entitled "Bibliography." Others prefer you follow the format of most sociology journals, listing only those materials actually cited in your paper; in this case, the list is entitled "References." Check with your instructor to see which type of listing is preferred, but remember that in *both* cases, you must list the source of all borrowed ideas, whether they are directly quoted or paraphrased.

When you are compiling your Bibliography or References section, list all sources alphabetically by the author's last name. Under each author's name, list works according to the year of publication, beginning with the most recent. Do not separate the list into sections for "articles," "books," and other sources; a single list is sufficient. Do not use italics, underlining, or abbreviations, other than "ed." for "editor," "trans." for "translator," "p." for "page," or "pp." for "pages." When typing this section, center the heading, putting it all in capital letters, and triple space between the heading and the first source listed.

When the source you have cited has more than one author, both or all the authors' names should be included, in the same order in which they appear on the book's title page or after the title of the article. Alphabetize under the first author's name. The first author should be listed last name first and the other author(s) should be listed first name first. (The format is illustrated below in the examples for journal articles.)

Use the examples below as models for capitalization, spacing, and punctuation of various kinds of source materials. For additional models, check the format of citations and reference entries in any issue of *American Sociological Review*. Here are some general tips.

1. Is the work a *book* whose entire main text is written by the same author or authors? If so, note that in this format titles of books are not underlined or italicized in the References or Bibliography list. If a book was first published many years ago, include the original publication date in brackets on the first line under the author's name, and the more recent date directly below it. For more than one book published in the same year by the same author(s), specify each as "a," "b," and so on.

Examples of Listings for Books

Durkheim, Emile
  [1897] Suicide. Glencoe, IL: Free Press.
  1951

Elias, Norbert
  [1939] The Civilizing Process, Volume 2: Power and Civil-
  1982   ity, Edmund Jephcott, trans., New York: Pantheon
          Books.

  1978a   The Civilizing Process, Volume 1: A History of Man-
          ners, Edmund Jephcott, trans., New York: Unizen
          Books.

  1978b   What Is Sociology? Stephen Mennell and Grace
          Morrissey, trans., New York: Columbia University
          Press.

Matza, David
  1969   Becoming Deviant. Englewood Cliffs, NJ: Prentice-
          Hall.

2. Is the work an *article* published in a *journal?* Note that only the
first letter of the first word of the article's title is capitalized. Give the
volume number of the issue in which the article appears, and the
season of publication if that is how the journal identifies its issues.
Give page numbers to help your readers locate the article.

Examples of Listings for Journal Articles

Mercy, James A. and Lala Carr Skelman
  1982   "Familial influence on the intellectual attainment in
          children." American Sociological Review 47:532–542.

Parnas, Raymond I.
  1967   "The police response to the domestic disturbance."
          Wisconsin Law Review 4 (Fall):914–960.

Yarrow, M., C. Schwartz, H. Murphy, and L. Deasy
  1955   "The psychological meaning of mental illness in the
          family." Journal of Social Issues 11:12–24.

3. Is the work found in a *collection of articles* which have been
edited into an anthology? If you are referring to a specific article in
the collection, the citation goes under the name of the author of the
article and includes the name of the anthology and the editor(s)
within the reference. Its capitalization and punctuation should follow
the format of a journal article, and here too you should include the
page numbers for your reader's convenience.

If you are referring to the anthology as a whole, the reference is
listed under the name of the editor(s). The format is like that of any
other book.

Examples of Listings for Collections

Conrad, Peter and Joseph W. Schneider
  1980   "Professionalization, monopoly, and the structure of
          medical practice." Pp. 155–165 in Peter Conrad and
          Rochelle Kern (eds.), The Sociology of Health and
          Illness, Critical Perspectives. New York: St. Martin's
          Press.

Emerson, Robert M. (ed.)
  1983   Contemporary Field Research. Boston and Toronto:
          Little, Brown.

Chapter 5

AVOIDING PLAGIARISM

Careful citation is important because plagiarism is burglary—cheating which presents another writer's words or ideas as if they were your own. Plagiarism is taken very seriously in colleges and universities and can be grounds for expulsion. You can avoid unintentional plagiarism by making careful notes that respect the integrity of the sources you are using, and by identifying exactly where you got borrowed words or ideas that you later use in your paper. You must cite the sources of both directly quoted words and paraphrased ideas.

Quoting a source directly means extracting a word, phrase, sentence, or passage, and inserting it, enclosed by double quotation marks or indented, according to its length, into your own paper. There are two minor changes you may make in a quotation, neither of which changes its meaning. These two legitimate changes are illustrated in our own quotation from C. Wright Mills' *The Sociological Imagination* (1959).

> Every individual lives from one generation to the next, in some society; . . . he [or she] lives out a biography, and . . . he lives it out with some historical sequence. By the fact of his living he

Thou shalt not steal.

O THE LONG ARM OF THE LAW

contributes, however minutely, to the shaping of his society and its history, even as he is made by society and by its historical push and shove. (6)

First, notice that we omit some of Mills' sentence, again without changing the meaning, and we indicate this omission by a punctuation mark called "ellipses," three dots. If the ellipsis points came at the end of the sentence, they would be followed by a period—hence four dots. Second, we are uneasy about Mills' use of "he" to refer to all humankind and want to make the language inclusive, so we add our own words "[or she]," inserting them within square brackets into Mills' quotation.

Another possible addition within square brackets is the Latin word *sic*, meaning "so," which you can use when you want to quote original words that contain an error. For example, in her paper at the end of Chapter 8, Sandra Ducoff Garber quotes her interview notes of a family member saying "I did the standard trick of look [*sic*] at his ear and not at his face which just drove him up the wall and he would get so frustrated and so angry."

Paraphrasing means condensing the author's meaning and translating a passage into your own words. This is a perfectly acceptable practice and, in fact, an important skill to develop. Paraphrasing forces you to think through and actively understand what you have read. But if you use another's idea when writing, you must give that person credit with a citation, even if you are presenting the idea in your own words.

There are good and bad ways to paraphrase. Here is an original passage from Emile Durkheim's *Suicide* (1951), followed by examples of good and bad paraphrasing.

The term "suicide" is applied to all cases of death resulting directly or indirectly from a positive or negative act of the victim himself, which he knows will produce this result.... This definition excludes from our study everything related to the suicide of animals. Our knowledge of animal intelligence does not really allow us to attribute to them an understanding anticipatory of their death nor, especially, of the means to accomplish it.... If some dogs refuse to take food on losing their masters, it is because the sadness into which they are thrown has automatically caused lack of hunger; death has resulted, but without having been foreseen.... So the special characteristics of suicide as defined by us are lacking. (44–45)

Here are two examples of bad paraphrasing. In the first, the writer has shifted words around in the sentences and replaced individual

words by plugging in synonyms. The writer has not genuinely condensed or translated the author's meaning into her or his own words;
this problem is usually compounded by a failure to cite the source (in
this case, Durkheim):

> When some pets stop eating because their owners have left, this
> is caused by the unhappiness into which they have fallen, which
> necessarily makes them lose their appetite: the final end that
> ensues, however, was not anticipated. Therefore, the unique fea-
> tures of suicide as described by our definition are missing.

In the second example, the writer has changed the order but kept
the words the same. Again the writer has not condensed the passage
or translated it into her or his own words; and, again, this problem is
usually compounded by a failure to cite the source:

> Lost masters cause their sad dogs, refusing food, to lack hunger.
> The dogs die, not foreseeing this result. What is lacking is our
> special characterization of suicide as we define it.

A good paraphrase boils down the original idea and puts it in your
own words. Here is a good paraphrase:

> *Example:* According to Durkheim (1951:44–45), animals, such as
> abandoned dogs who starve themselves, do not commit suicide
> because they do not understand the connection between death
> and the means of causing death.

Remember that even good paraphrasing requires citing the source
of the borrowed *idea* being presented.

PART II

WRITING FROM VARIOUS DATA SOURCES

As to Holmes, I observed that he sat frequently for half an hour on end, with knitted brows and an abstracted air, but he swept the matter away with a wave of his hand when I mentioned it. "Data! data! data!" he cried impatiently. "I can't make bricks without clay."

DR. WATSON IN CONAN DOYLE'S
"Adventure of the Copper Beeches"

The goal of a sociology paper is to develop a thesis in response to a question about the social world and to support that thesis with evidence. But where does the evidence come from?

There is no one answer. As we indicated earlier, sociology is diverse. Data may be gathered from many sources, by several methods. The next four chapters present guidelines for writing papers based on four data sources—library research, textual analysis, ethnographic field research, and quantitative research. They reflect the most typical writing assignments in sociology classes, and use or modify the formats described earlier: essay and journal (see Chapter 1). Three of the four chapters can be used from the first day of your first sociology class. Since quantitative research, however, depends on specialized ways of collecting and analyzing information, the last chapter will be more useful if you are taking or have taken a basic course in quantitative methods.

An annotated sample paper, written by an undergraduate sociology student, concludes each chapter except the one on library research.

The sample papers illustrate our guidelines. You can match them up with your own papers and use our marginal comments to check what you have written yourself.

Rather than include a sample library research paper in this section, we have instead presented information about specialized sociology reference sources. There are two reasons for this substitution. First, we have found that students are more likely, from their previous English classes, to be familiar with the library research paper than with the other kinds of papers assigned in sociology. Second, to some extent the sample paper which follows Chapter 1 can be considered a library research paper, insofar as the author had to use the library to get supporting evidence; consult it if you want to see how bibliographic materials are incorporated into an essay.

You will find the guidelines for using library references very valuable, particularly those on *Sociological Abstracts* and the *Social Science Citation Index*, since these are keys to the vast sociological literature in the library. Although our list of reference sources is not exhaustive, it will get you started in the right direction.

Papers often require you to do some library research even when data are drawn primarily from another source. For example, quantitative research papers entail reviewing the literature, which means going to the library. Since this section can be helpful for proceeding in the others, we begin with how to do a library research paper.

Chapter 6

THE LIBRARY RESEARCH PAPER

A library research paper requires you to use the library in two ways: first, to develop the question that you will address in your paper if it hasn't been assigned; and, second, to collect the information that you will use to support your paper's thesis. In order to prepare your paper, you must know how to ask a good sociological question (see Chapter 1) and how to use the library effectively. Most library research papers require the following steps.

Scheduling Your Time

Work backward with your time grid (see Chapter 2), making deadlines for stages in your project, such as choosing a topic, beginning research, recording information, organizing an outline, drafting the paper, revising it, and writing the final version.

Scheduling your time is important with a library research paper because if your library doesn't have crucial books and articles, you will have to order them through a service (often free) called interlibrary loan. Interlibrary loan is a way to borrow books temporarily from other libraries. Your own college librarian can usually arrange for this service if you need to read material which is not in your library. But the interlibrary loan service takes time. Therefore you must start working on the project as soon as possible to allow time for all the steps and, if necessary, to allow time to order and get material.

Before You Go to the Library: Choosing a Topic

You often start a library research project not knowing much about your topic. How, then, do you begin to develop a good question?

First, you must select a general subject area—an area that is rele-

vant to the concerns of your course and of interest to you. One way to
find a topic is to skim your syllabus and course readings. Be sure to
consider the entire syllabus, since a topic that will be discussed later
in the course might be the basis for a good research question. Your
instructor can help at this stage by letting you know if your topic is
too broad or too far afield.

Next, even before going to the library, construct some provisional
questions. For example, let's say you want to study the feminist movement in the United States. Ask yourself why this topic interests you.
Your personal interest in a subject not only motivates you during the
research and writing process; it can also guide you to ask a good
question. Also ask yourself what specific aspect of the subject you
want to investigate for this particular class assignment, and what
specifically you want to know about it. In the case of feminism, for
example, you may want to focus your research on differences in wages
(such as, "Are women's wages lower than men's?"), on power differences (such as, "Why do unequal power relations exist between men
and women?"), or on ways people learn to fill the gender roles expected of them (such as, "How are males and females socialized to
enact sex role stereotypes in their daily lives?").

Remember to maintain a sociological perspective on the subject.
The examples given in the previous paragraph, for instance, are sociologically relevant because they are concerned with differences between groups of people (men and women) and because they focus on
patterned relationships in the social world. A review of Chapter 1 will
help stimulate the sociological imagination you need to ask a good
question.

Once you have narrowed your topic and begun to shape it into a
question, it's time to go to the library.

Using the Library to Review the Sociological Literature

Begin your work in the library by getting an overview of the sociological research which has already been conducted into your question. (The
"Locating References" section that follows will help you in this.) This
overview of research published in books and journal articles is called
"a review of the literature." ("Literature" in this sense, of course, has
nothing to do with fiction and poetry.) "Reviewing the literature" in
sociology involves discovering whether scholarly research has been
published on the question you tentatively have in mind, how the question was formulated, and what answers have been suggested.

Reviewing the literature will help you in two important and interrelated ways. First, a review of the literature helps you to refine your question. How has the question been framed before? Has more than one plausible answer been suggested as a result of empirical or theoretical research? Remember as you fine-tune your question that you must be able to find sufficient evidence to support the answer you will propose, and that it must be specific enough to be researchable within the time frame of your assignment. Second, reviewing the literature helps you to identify those books and journal articles which contain reports of research into the question you are addressing in your paper. The quality of your paper will depend on how thoroughly you locate such research; it is the "data" you will use to support your thesis. Once you locate relevant books and articles, you will take in-depth notes on them.

Locating Specialized Sociological References

The key to the library is the reference section. The reference librarians are there to answer your questions and help you find the appropriate books, articles, journals, and abstracts for your project.

If your course textbooks include sections on "Recommended Reading," often located at the ends of chapters, you can start with those references, choosing suggested books and articles that seem most appropriate. Start with the most recently published sources because they include references to earlier works.

Be aware that, unlike most papers for high school, for a college research paper you will be expected to consult articles in specialized professional journals. In the last section of this chapter you will find an annotated list of journals commonly used by sociologists.

In addition to any references you find in your texts, you should begin your research with the following five library resources on which sociology students rely:

- *Catalog*
- *Sociological Abstracts*
- *Social Science Citation Index*
- *Social Science Index*
- *International Encyclopedia of the Social Sciences*

Catalog

Use the catalog to find suitable books in your library. Library books may be identified on index cards in drawers. Or books may be listed on celluloid microfiches which you must read in special machines to magnify this information. Or your library may catalog its books with a computerized system which displays this information on a screen; and with some computerized online systems you can print out your own copy of appropriate information. In all three cases, only the equipment changes; the books are organized in the same way—according to author's name, title, and subject.

Finding information by looking in the catalog under author and title is relatively straightforward. But if you look under a subject for books about your topic and don't find any information, it may be because the subject you are looking under is not an official subject category. For example, if you look in the catalog under "Coping," you will not find anything. "Coping" is not an official topic. In this case, you must consult a special reference book to find official topics (called "subject headings"). This special reference book is a large red two-volume set called *The Library of Congress Subject Headings* and is usually placed near the catalog. For example, if you look up "Coping" in *The Library of Congress Subject Headings*, you will find these instructions:

Coping. *See* Adjustment (Psychology).

That means that you should look under "Adjustment (Psychology)" in the catalog to find books on coping. As another example, if you want to find books on fraternities, *The Library of Congress Subject Headings* tells you to look in the catalog under the official topic "Greek letter societies."

Sociological Abstracts

This reference is published as a set of volumes each year. *Sociological Abstracts* gives more than bibliographic information. It also provides abstracts of articles published in major sociological journals. (An abstract is a summary of an article.) Learning to use *Sociological Abstracts* will save you much time, since these summaries will allow you to decide whether the sources themselves are relevant to your topic. In this way you can weed some out without having to locate and read them.

To use *Sociological Abstracts*, follow these two steps:

Step One Locate the index volume for a recent year. Here you will find subject headings. Under the headings will be references to abstracts. Each abstract has its own unique number. For example, under the subject heading of "Mental illness/Mentally ill" you will find the information shown in Figure 6-1. Jot down the number at the end of any references to abstracts that look potentially useful, for example, N7474. These numbers are not page numbers. They are abstract numbers. Each abstract, in another volume, has its own number, like N7474.

Figure 6-1 Index Entry from *Sociological Abstracts*

Mental illness/Mentally ill
accommodation processes, informal treatment of mental illness; case study data collected by students; troublesome individuals not receiving formal treatment; N7474
health breakdown, mental/phyical illness susceptibility; social support insufficiency/disruption; N7412
inferences of mental illness; social noninvolvement; experiment, videotapes; college students; N7392
medical/sociological characteristics of pronoia/paranoia; comments, reply; N7459

Step Two Now look up the abstract by its number in a separate volume which is usually shelved next to the index volume. This abstract will give a summary of the article and bibliographic information telling you where the complete article can be found. Papers delivered at conferences are also summarized in the abstracts. When using the abstracts, make sure you are aware of the sources of articles, since it may be very difficult for you to find papers that are delivered at conferences and have not been published. For example, if your topic is on accommodation processes, then you would look up the number N7474 and find the abstract shown in Figure 6-2. The bibliographic information indicates that this article was published in the journal *Social Problems*, which is found in most libraries. If you already have

Figure 6-2 Text Entry from *Sociological Abstracts*

84 = 1984
N 7474 = abstract number

84N7474

Lynch, Michael (School Social Sciences U California, Irvine 92717), **Accommodation Practices: Vernacular Treatments of Madness, UM** *Social Problems*, 1983, 31, 2, Dec, 152–164.

¶ Commitment to mental hospitals normally follows a period of informal attempts at accommodation by family & friends. The nature of these accommodation processes is examined on the basis of data collected for term papers by students in classes on the sociology of mental illness; each paper described a person who, though not classified as mentally ill, was a persistent source of trouble for others, & also described the accommodation processes used in coping with the troublesome behavior. Three classes of accommodation practices are identified: minimizing contact by avoiding or ignoring the troublemaker; managing the troublemaker's actions by humoring, screening, taking over, orienting to a varying level of normality, & practical jokes & retaliations; & influencing reactions to the troublemaker, including producing notoriety, shadowing, giving advance warning, hiding & diluting the troublemaker; & covering up. These processes reveal the role of groups & organizations in constructing normality. 24 References. Modified HA

Figure 6-3 Index Entry from *Sociological Abstracts*

> Lyman, Stanford M., N7208, N7240
> Lynch, Michael, N7474
> Lynn, Richard, N8361

an author's name and want an abstract of the article, you can start looking in the index volume under authors' names, not subject headings (see Figure 6-3). Locating N7474 is the same as step 2 above.

It is helpful to go through these indexes by annual volume in order to become familiar with new published sources for your research. At the end of each year, a cumulative index is compiled that you can refer to and save time by not having to search through each individual volume.

Social Science Citation Index

This annual, multivolume work, like *Sociological Abstracts*, provides bibliographic information. But *Social Science Citation Index* gives other information and is a unique and invaluable reference source for undergraduates and established scholars alike. Its main special feature is the way it identifies the references that authors cite in their own articles (hence the word "citation" in its title). This feature allows you to trace the interconnected network of a research tradition and see which scholars' work influenced which other scholars. Two other features of the work enable you to find information through key words in titles and by authors' academic or corporate affiliation. Because so much information, often abbreviated, is compressed into this source, and the print is quite small, do not expect to find the *Social Science Citation Index* easy to decipher and read. However, with some examples, like the ones to follow to guide you in understanding its organization, and with some brief experience using it, you will find the *Social Science Citation Index* an indispensable reference tool.

Each annual set of the complete *Social Science Citation Index* includes these four volumes:

- *Source Index*
- *Citation Index*
- *Subject Index*
- *Corporate Index*

To use the *Social Science Citation Index* follow these corresponding four steps:

Step One Look in a recent year's *Source Index* to find bibliographic information about current work by a particular author, for example, Michael Lynch, a scholar cited in the sample ethnographic field research paper in Chapter 8. Figure 6-4, an entry from the 1984 *Source*

Figure 6-4 *Source Index* Entry, *Social Science Citation Index*

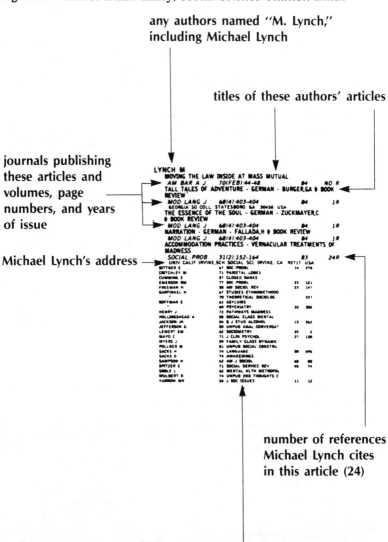

any authors named "M. Lynch,"
including Michael Lynch

titles of these authors' articles

journals publishing
these articles and
volumes, page
numbers, and years
of issue

Michael Lynch's address

number of references
Michael Lynch cites
in this article (24)

information about Michael Lynch's 24 citations (including cited
authors' names, years of publication of cited sources, titles of
cited sources, and volume and beginning page numbers of cited
journal articles)

Index, provides information on the current work of anyone identified as M. Lynch, including this Michael Lynch. The information is abbreviated and often requires some detective work to decipher and confirm by cross-checking. From this list you can tell that in his article "Accommodation Practices: Vernacular Treatments of Madness," M. Lynch (who's really Michael Lynch) cites 24 other sources, including, for example, an article by E. M. Lemert, published in 1962 in a journal entitled *Sociometry,* volume 25, beginning on page 2.

Step Two Look in that year's *Citation Index* to find articles that cite earlier known works by a particular author. Use this volume to go from older publications to the more recent, related articles that cite them (see Figure 6-5). By cross-checking this information with *Sociological Abstracts* and with the *Source Index* in *Social Science Citation Index,* you can establish that one of these references is to the Michael Lynch who wrote "Accommodation Practices: Vernacular Treatments of Madness," but that the other references are to other authors named "M. Lynch." For example, the reference in bold type to "83 AM WAY MAR 64" refers to an article by Mitchell Lynch titled "Hard-Nosing in Academe," published in a journal called *American Way,* in March

Figure 6-5 *Citation Index* **Entry,** *Social Science Citation Index*

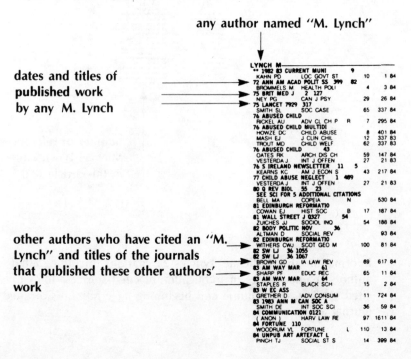

1983. This article by Mitchell Lynch in *American Way* is cited by Robert Staples in Staples' article "Racial Ideology and Intellectual Racism: Blacks in Academia," published in *The Black Scholar*, volume 15, beginning on page 2 of the March–April issue, 1984. But the last item on this list turns out to be by the same M. Lynch who wrote the article on "Accommodation Practices." This last reference, "84 UN-PUB ART ARTEFACT L," when it's tracked down, turns out to refer to a book by Michael Lynch, *Art and Artefact in Laboratory Science: A Study of Shop Work and Shop Talk in a Research Laboratory*, which was then in press and not published until 1985. Lynch's book is cited in an article by Trevor J. Pinch and Wiebe E. Bijker, "The Social Construction of Facts and Artefacts: Or, How the Sociology of Science and the Sociology of Technology Might Benefit Each Other," published in *Social Studies of Science*, volume 14, beginning on page 399 of the August 1984 issue.

Step Three Look in the year's *Subject Index* to find articles which have words of interest in their titles. (If you find anything appropriate, then you can find full information about the author[s] in the *Source Index*, step 1.) See Figure 6-6 for an example. From this list you can tell that M. Lynch used the words "Treatments" and "Vernacular" in a title or titles of his published work.

Step Four Look in the year's *Corporate Index* to find articles if you know some corporate or academic institution publishes work on a topic. From the list in Figure 6-7 you can tell in which journals the members of the School of Social Sciences at the University of California, Irvine, including M. Lynch, published recent articles.

Social Science Index

This index identifies where and when journal articles on social science topics have been published. The index does not print articles. Instead, it tells you which issue of the journal to look in for the article itself. The information is abbreviated, and the abbreviations are explained at the beginning of each volume. You will also find titles of indexed journals at the beginning of each volume.

The index lists information about articles in two ways, by author's name and by subject headings followed by a list of relevant articles. You can therefore search for information in two ways.

If you know the author's name, look it up in the index by year to see what he or she has published. If you know the year of the publication, simply get the index for that year and look up the author's name. The listings are in alphabetical order. For example, if you are looking for a source citation of an article written by Emerson and Messinger in 1977, pull out the 1977 index and look under Emerson. You will find the information shown in Figure 6-8. This information is abbreviated,

Figure 6-6 *Subject Index* **Entry,** *Social Science Citation Index*

general subject (Madness)

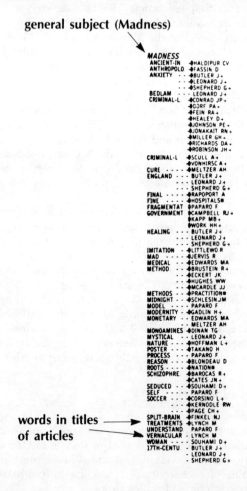

words in titles —
of articles —

and by checking the abbreviations at the beginning of the volume you will be able to establish that Robert M. Emerson and Sheldon L. Messinger published an article, "The Micropolitics of Trouble," on pages 121–134 in volume 25 of the journal *Social Problems*, published in December 1977.

You can also look under subject headings for issues and titles of articles connected with your topic. For example, if you look up "Mentally Ill" in the 1977–78 index, you will find the references to subsections shown in Figure 6-9. By demonstrating a range of topics, the subsections can help you determine which specific aspect of mental

Figure 6-7 *Corporate Index* Entry, *Social Science Citation Index*

CALIFORNIA

IRVINE

institution ——➤ • UNIV CALIF IRVINE

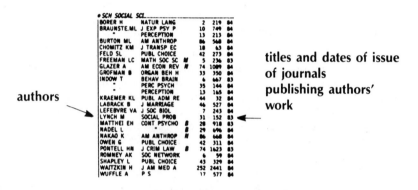

Figure 6-8 Author's Name, *Social Science Index*

Emerson, Robert M. and Messinger, Sheldon L.
Micro-politics of trouble. bibl Soc Prob 25:121-34 D '77

Figure 6-9 Subject Entry, *Social Science Index*

Mentally ill
See also
Aged—Mental illness
Delinquents—Mental illness
Emotionally disturbed
Mental illness
Mentally handicapped—Mental illness
Mentally handicapped children—Mental illness
Neuroses
Physicians—Mental illness
Psychiatrists—Mental illness
Veterans—Mental illness
Women—Mental illness
Youth—Mental illness

illness you are most interested in researching, as well as giving you a sample of references you can begin to read. For example, if you look up the subject heading "Social interaction" in the index, you will find another reference to this same article, "Micropolitics of Trouble," as shown in Figure 6-10.

Figure 6-10 Subject Entry, *Social Science Index*

Social interaction

Measurement of role identity. P. J. Burke and J. C. Tully. bibl
    Soc Forces 55:881-97 Je '77
Micro-politics of trouble. R. M. Emerson and S. L. Messinger.
    bibl Soc Prob 25:121-34 D '77
Mirroring: one vehicle to organizational clarity. L Cooper. Int
    J Soc Psych 22:288-95 Wint '76-77

International Encyclopedia of the Social Sciences

This source explains key terms and concepts, and provides background information on the life and times of key figures in the history
of the social sciences. For example, if you look up the term "alienation," you will find a definition of the term and a discussion of the
different ways that Hegel, Marx, and Weber presented this concept in
their writings. A bibliography is also given in each entry, but it is not
as up-to-date as what you will find in the catalog, abstracts, or
indexes.

A Note on Computerized Literature Search

You may be able to take advantage of computer technology to find
appropriate bibliographic information. There are two ways students
can tap into many data bases, including the reference sources mentioned above. First, your own college library may be able to do a
computerized literature search for you. In that case, begin by asking a
reference librarian about the possibility and cost of this service. Or,
second, if you (or your family or dorm) have access to a personal
computer and a modem, you can use a commercial online information
retrieval service such as Knowledge Index or BRS/After Dark. Again,
your own college reference librarian will probably be able to give you
information.

Recording Information

Index cards are a handy tool for gathering two kinds of information:
bibliographic information on the sources you consult and the ideas
you borrow from these sources.
   Bibliography cards: Make one bibliography card for each source (see
Figures 6-11 and 6-12, for examples). Include on this card the following information in this order:

> Author: all authors of the work with surnames and first names
>   in inverted order
> Title: article, chapter, or book
> Facts of publication:
>   *For journals:* journal name in full, date of publication,
>   volume number, inclusive pages.
>   *For books:* city of publication, publisher's name, publication date.

Take this list and the examples with you to the library so that the
bibliography cards you write will be complete. You will need all the
above information when you cite your sources later in your paper. So
write down this information when it's easy to do so, that is, when
you have the source in front of you—and avoid wasting valuable
time backtracking. Later you will be able to shuffle these bibliography
cards into alphabetical order, based on authors' surnames, and
in this way prepare the last page(s) of your paper (see Chapter 4). A
variation on the note card system is to use a looseleaf binder and
looseleaf paper. This allows shuffling and ordering, just as index
cards do. Software companies are also beginning to develop and
market comparable programs, like "3 X 5," that can be used on a
personal computer.

Note cards: You make note cards for two reasons: to support your
memory while thinking about a topic and to shape data into usable

Figure 6-11 Example of a Bibliography Card for a Journal Article

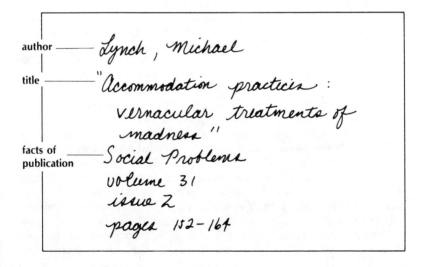

author ——— Lynch, Michael

title ——— "Accommodation practices:
            vernacular treatments of
            madness"

facts of ——— Social Problems
publication
            volume 31
            issue 2
            pages 152-164

Figure 6-12 Example of a Bibliography Card for a Book

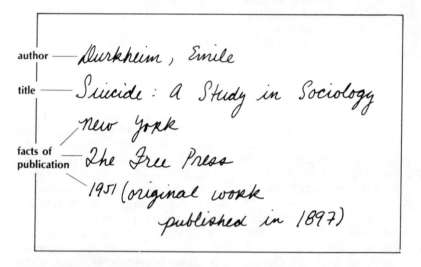

author — Durkheim, Emile

title — Suicide: A Study in Sociology

facts of
publication — New York
The Free Press
1951 (original work
published in 1897)

form. The physical act of recording on cards loads the data into your mind very efficiently, so that you can retrieve them in manageable chunks as you consolidate your own answer to your research question. Note cards also help you avoid problems of parroting and unintentional plagiarism. Parroting means mechanically repeating sources without any sign of your own thinking; for information about the serious offense of plagiarism, see Chapter 5.

Limit each note card to one piece of information from a single article or book. You may quote exact words from the original, or you may paraphrase these ideas. Paraphrase means summarize the idea in your own words (see Chapter 5). *Remember to include specific page references* to words and ideas that you record on your note cards as you write them. You will need this information later.

Look for two kinds of information to record on note cards: (1) main concepts related to your research question, and (2) any particularly interesting supporting details. "Interesting" means interesting to you—details that stick in your mind as you read because they connect with your own academic or personal experience.

Label each note card with a subject heading of your own at the top. Try to come up with a description which is precise without copying out the whole note again. You will depend on these subject headings later to group your note cards and sort them into piles. These piles will be the basis for a provisional outline for your paper. At the bottom of each note card, identify the source of your borrowed idea. You can abbreviate this information on a note card because you already have a complete record on a bibliography card. Remember to include the specific page number.

What exactly are you looking for in your note-taking? In some ways, you can think of this part of your work as asking questions not unlike those you would pose in a textual analysis (see Chapter 7). Your notes should indicate answers to the key questions about the article or book you are reading: What major question is the author addressing in this work? Why does the author think the question is important to sociological theory or to the world at large? What methods did the researcher use to try to answer the question and/or what work of others is cited to make a significant point? What thesis does the author propose in response to the question? What evidence does he or she use to support the answer?

As you take notes you will see that there is no one answer to your research question. It is not a matter of finding the truth, but of tracing the main issues raised in regard to the question, the main answers proposed, and the main disagreements among those engaged in the field. Eventually you will use these notes to explain in your paper why you believe one answer to be more convincing than the others which have been suggested.

When you first start your project you may find yourself making quite a few note cards because the subject is often new to you. However, as you read more, and become more informed, you will be narrowing down the answer to your question. At the same time your thesis will be emerging more clearly in your own mind, and you will be selecting subsequent readings more deliberately. As the material becomes familiar you will likely take fewer notes per reading. This process of adjustment and refinement happens almost automatically.

Here is an original passage from Emile Durkheim's book *Suicide* (1951:168); Figure 6-13 shows one sample note card based on the passage:

As a rule suicide increases with knowledge. Knowledge does not determine this progress. It is innocent; nothing is more unjust than to accuse it. . . . But these two facts result simultaneously from a single general state which they translate into different forms. Man seeks to learn and man kills himself because of the loss of cohesion in his religious society; he does not kill himself because of his learning. It is certainly not the learning he acquires that disorganizes religion; but the desire for knowledge wakens because religion becomes disorganized. Knowledge is not sought as a means to destroy accepted opinions but because their destruction has commenced.

Figure 6-13 Example of a Note Card

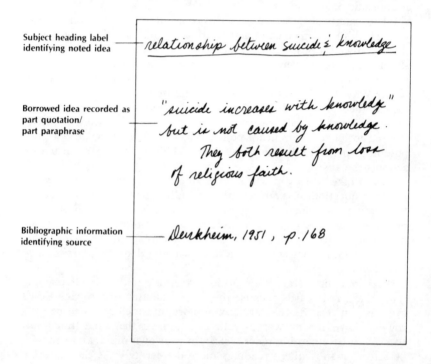

Subject heading label
identifying noted idea

Borrowed idea recorded as
part quotation/
part paraphrase

Bibliographic information
identifying source

Remember to include on your note cards the page number(s) of quotations and paraphrased ideas. Otherwise you may later have to skim the entire source just to locate the page for a passage you want to cite.

Looking Deeper

Now that you are immersed in your topic, you can use the materials that you have found to direct you to further books and articles which may be useful to you. As you are engaged in taking notes, make bibliographical cards for any references in your reading which seem relevant to your topic. You may discover these in the body of the work itself or in the References at the end. The catalog (for books) and serials list (for periodical literature such as journal articles) will help you again in locating these references in your library.

Organizing Your Information

Once you have finished making note cards, reread them in any order to get an overview of your information. You should now be able to state your thesis, which these notes support, very clearly. With your thesis in mind, sort your note cards into piles, according to the subject headings you gave them. This shuffling will not necessarily be neat, but you will be distinguishing separate main points and preparing the basis for an outline.

Matching Thesis, Note Cards, and Outline

Decide on the main point in each pile of note cards and make that a main point on an outline. Use the detailed information in the pile to elaborate this main point.

You may find that some of your note cards no longer fit the final version of your thesis. If so, abandon them. Including irrelevant information, even though you worked hard to get it, will distract your reader, weaken your argument, and count against you.

In order to decide on a sequence of main points—that is, which main point to start with and what order to follow with the others—think of your reader. What order will be the most convincing? What order of main points will best support your thesis? Then use each main point as the basis of a different paragraph. Use details from your piles of note cards to build up each paragraph, presenting your sequence of thoughts in a logical pattern with transitions marking the movement of your argument (see Chapter 10 for more information on transitions). In the concluding section, summarize your major findings. Here you can also briefly refer to other related issues or topics that merit further investigation.

Major Journals Often Used by Sociologists

Scholars rely on journal articles, as well as books, to keep up with new research and professional opinion. But journals aren't a trade secret. Undergraduates, who are apprentice scholars, can also use them. Most college libraries have a special quiet, convenient place where current issues of major journals are kept before being bound and shelved, like other books, in the main sections of the library. We recommend that you find this reading area, often called "Current Periodicals," and browse through some of the journals listed below. This experience will give you a dramatic sense of the discipline's ongoing research tradition, which is only hinted at in textbooks. It may also trigger some ideas about possible topics for your own future papers. Although the articles in these journals are intended primarily for a trained scholarly audience, rather than the general public, and sometimes employ sophisticated statistical techniques, you will find many articles easily accessible to undergraduates.

American Journal of Sociology: Published bimonthly by the University of Chicago Press, this influential journal includes theoretical and research articles, book reviews, and commentaries on articles published previously.

American Sociological Review: Published bimonthly by the American Sociological Association (ASA), this review covers diverse areas of sociology, often with a statistical and empirical orientation. A cumulative index appears every three years.

Annual Review of Sociology: These review articles, which summarize some particular field of sociology, reflect a broad perspective and can be found under such categories as differentiation and stratification, institutions, political and economic sociology, social processes, policy, historical sociology, urban sociology, and political sociology.

British Journal of Sociology: Published quarterly, this journal discusses historical and theoretical as well as methodological issues. An annual index also includes book reviews.

Contemporary Sociology: Published bimonthly by the ASA, its special feature is to review books, journals, articles, and films, covering a wide range of areas such as historical and comparative sociology, social psychology, gender, education, and stratification. The review essays are especially useful for learning about new publications and sociologists' evaluations of them.

Criminology: Published quarterly, this interdisciplinary journal emphasizes research about crime and deviant behavior within the social and behavioral sciences and presents articles on the theoretical and historical components of crime, law, and criminal justice.

Journal of Health and Social Behavior: Published quarterly by the ASA, it uses a sociological perspective in understanding health-related issues, for example, organizational aspects of hospitals or class characteristics of sufferers from various illnesses.

Journal of Marriage and the Family: Published quarterly by the National Council on Family Relations, it covers such diverse research areas as family planning, family structure, theories of the family, and cross-cultural studies on fertility. Each issue also features a book review section.

Journal of Social Issues: Published quarterly by the Society for Psychological Study of Social Issues, it groups articles on similar subjects, all reflecting a psychological perspective on social issues within communities.

Rural Sociology: Published quarterly, this is the official journal of the Rural Sociological Society.

Social Forces: Published quarterly, this journal for social research and methodology presents articles on such topics as mobility, class, ethnicity, gender, and education. Each issue includes book reviews.

Social Problems: Published five times yearly, this is the official journal of the Society for the Study of Social Problems.

Social Psychology Quarterly: Published quarterly by the ASA, it covers empirical and theoretical studies related to social interaction, socialization, labeling, conformity, and attitudes.

Social Science Quarterly: It features book reviews, forums, research notes, and articles concerned with social issues, including such topics as race and ethnicity, family migration, and criminology.

Sociological Inquiry: Published quarterly for the chapters of the Alpha Kappa Delta (the Undergraduate Sociology Honors Society), it covers a wide range of sociological topics.

Sociological Methods and Research: Published quarterly, it covers research in methodological, quantitative, and empirical issues in the field of sociology, and also includes review articles.

Sociological Quarterly: This journal presents research on recent theoretical, methodological, and empirical developments in the field of sociology.

Sociological Review: Published quarterly in England, this interdisciplinary journal presents a range of sociological topics such as social mobility and class structure, and includes book reviews.

Sociology and Social Research: Published quarterly, this journal's interdisciplinary approach is reflected in its research articles, review articles, and book reviews.

Urban Life: Published quarterly, it presents ethnographic studies based on qualitative interviewing and participant observation.

This list is not exhaustive. For more references to specialized journals and governmental sources, ask your reference librarian or consult

Bart, Pauline and Linda Frankel.
1985 The Student Sociologist's Handbook. 4th ed. New York: Random House.

For additional general information about writing library research papers, we recommend

Hubbuch, Susan M.
1985 Writing Research Papers Across the Curriculum. New York: Holt, Rinehart and Winston.

Lester, James D.
  1985 Writing Research Papers: A Complete Guide. 4th ed. Glenview, IL: Scott, Foresman.

Strenski, Ellen and Madge Manfred.
  1985 The Research Paper Workbook. 2d ed. New York: Longman.

Chapter 7

THE TEXTUAL
ANALYSIS PAPER

You may be assigned a paper asking you to analyze a book or portion of a book—for example, Max Weber's *The Protestant Ethic and the Spirit of Capitalism* or Erving Goffman's *The Presentation of Self in Everyday Life.* We call this method "textual" analysis because the text itself, what the author wrote, provides your data. Your paper is an "analysis" because you take the author's work apart to examine the different components and then put them back together. This activity is called "explication"; a textual analysis explicates, or explains, what the author's main points are and how they are connected, and offers a critique of the author's argument. An analogy would be taking a car engine apart, explaining each part and how the parts work together, and evaluating whether the car is a good buy or a lemon.

Mastering the skill of explication will help you write better papers when a textual analysis is assigned. But, perhaps as important, this skill will help you evaluate more clearly all the books and articles you encounter in your academic career.

Asking Questions About the Text

In textual analysis, the text is not only your data but also the source of your question. That is, your question will arise from the author's ideas and arguments presented in the text and your analysis of them. Your question is a vehicle for conversing with the author about the thesis or argument of the work. This conversation should be conducted in an analytically critical manner, which means that to carry on your end you must raise questions about the logic of the argument, the type and credibility of the evidence, the soundness of the conclusion, and the fundamental assumptions on which the argument rests.

Your assignment may specify how you are to analyze a text, or the format may be left up to you. Here are three main kinds of questions generally addressed in a textual analysis:

What is the author saying? How well is it supported?

These are the basic questions in textual analysis. They involve considering: what is the author's main point(s)? Does the author support her or his claims with convincing evidence?

Depending on the assignment, these questions can be sufficient in themselves for developing a textual analysis or they may be used in special ways, as the next two categories illustrate.

How does this author deal with one important sociological concept or issue in this text?

Rather than analyzing all the ideas which the author presents, in this approach you focus in depth on one significant aspect of the text. If you are reading Talcott Parsons' book on the *Evolution of Societies*, for example, you might ask how Parsons views modern society. In that case, your questions would include: How does Parsons define "modern society"? Why, in light of the overall purpose of the book, does he discuss modern society? What evidence does he use to support his claims about it?

How does one text compare or contrast with another?

Compare-and-contrast assignments are probably the most common. If you are asked to compare and/or contrast two authors' works (or two works by the same author), you must start by identifying the common topic under consideration and use that as the basis for your question. How do these two works deal with an issue which is central to each? For example, the sample student paper in this chapter compares and contrasts Parsons' *Evolution of Societies* with Herbert Marcuse's *One-Dimensional Man*. The student writer chose to frame her question around Parsons' and Marcuse's views of modern society because that is a central focus of their work.

Any or all of these questions may be relevant to the particular work you are considering. Before you decide which questions will form the basis of your paper, you must read the text—and you must read it in a special way. We recommend that you buy your own copy of the book you will be using, if it is affordable. You will then be able to mark it up. Ellen Berlfein, author of the sample textual analysis paper at the end of this chapter, told us, "As I read the books I underlined things that were applicable to my question, and I used these underlined statements as the resource for my quotations."

How to Read the Text

Before developing your question, get to know the text. As you read, keep in mind three general tasks. First, you must *identify the main points* that are explicitly presented as parts of the argument. Second, you must *identify the author's hidden assumptions*—that is, what she or he takes for granted about how the world works, and does not question or bother to justify. To extend the car analogy, these assumptions are like the principles of physics taken for granted in building an engine. Third, you must *evaluate* the text, asking, for example, in what ways the argument is not convincing. What are its problems? How could it be better? Evaluating the argument is like diagnosing which engine parts do not work and how they could work, or arguing that the whole thing should be junked and stating why.

In other words, as you read you must ask yourself and ask the text the same sorts of questions that you will address in your paper. Here is a more detailed description of the close reading required for textual analysis:

Getting to Know Something About the Text

Here are some things you must find out in order to become acquainted with the text:

Who is the author? What is her or his background? This information is sometimes included in the introduction of the book. If there is no biographical information in the introduction, or if the information is insufficient to give you a picture of the author, there are resources you can use to find out the information.

The *Biography and Genealogy Master Index* contains a list of authors' names, followed by a list of references in which you will find biographical information. The reference book titles are abbreviated; consult the front of the book for the complete titles.

Information on well-known authors—for example, the founders of the discipline—might also be found in *Encyclopaedia Britannica, Encyclopedia Americana*, or the *International Encyclopedia of the Social Sciences.*

When was the text written? What was the social climate of the period? To determine when the text was written look at the copyright date in the front of the book. If you find more than one date, the first one indicates the date of the original printing or first edition. To determine the historical period in which the text was written look first to your introduction. If this does not provide adequate information, you can use the sources above, paying particular attention to the historical information given in entries on the author or the countries where the author lived.

What is the polemical context—that is, where is the text located in the ongoing debate on the question? To whom is the author responding? Sometimes the text will reveal the polemical context by explicitly contrasting the author's argument with other perspectives. This information may be found either in the body of the text or in the preface or introduction. Sometimes it requires reading between the lines, paying attention to how the author refers to other works, for example, by drawing contrasts between her or his position and that of others. If the polemical context is not obvious, look for other books or journal articles about the author or the subject of the text. Often scholars write critiques or commentaries on others' work, especially if it is controversial or considered exemplary This literature can be found in the library. (See Chapter 6 for guidelines about specific references.) Remember, the reference librarian can help you locate sources to help you get the information you need to write your paper.

Reading Twice

Read the text twice, for different purposes.

First, read for the big picture—get a feel for the text's organization and content. The author has major points that you are looking for. These major points, in turn, are supported by minor points. Pay special attention to the author's introduction, often called a preface, or to a foreword, written by an expert in the field.

After you have completed this preliminary reading, focus on the kind of question you will be addressing in your paper. If your instructor has specified a question, now is the time to consider it carefully and be sure you understand what information to provide, how deeply to analyze the work, and how much of your own opinion to give. If the assignment is more general, look back over the categories of questions we listed above and decide which approach you will take: Will you analyze the text as a whole? Would you rather focus on a particular concept or aspect of the argument? Or should you compare this work to another one?

With your question in mind, read the text very closely the second time through; this reading forms the core of your "data collection." Your goal is to understand the interconnected points that constitute the author's argument and to record these important points on note cards. Note-taking during this second reading is an important step toward writing your paper. We will deal with it in detail below.

What are you looking for in this detailed reading? Look for the author's argument—that is, the question that the author is trying to answer and the evidence she or he used to answer it. The following questions will assist you in identifying the text's argument, that is, the author's main points and the assumptions hidden beneath them:

• What is the author's question? For example, in *One-Dimensional Man*, Herbert Marcuse asks how capitalism affects freedom in a modern society.
• What is the author's answer—that is, what provides the core of the argument? What answers have other scholars given? Marcuse ar-

gues that capitalist technology limits individual freedom. In contrast, other theorists have argued that capitalism increases individual freedom.

- What evidence does the author offer to support this answer? Is the evidence logical or empirical or both? Does the evidence actually support the argument?
- How does the author get from point A to point B? How do the main points that you identified in your reading relate to one another?
- What are the assumptions? What does the author take for granted, points without which the argument could not be made? Some examples of fundamental assumptions are that people have free will, that our social order constitutes the normal state of affairs, or that free enterprise benefits everyone.

As you engage in this second reading, you may want to adjust your question. If you planned on analyzing the text as a whole, for example, you may now discover that for this particular paper that task is too broad. If you attempt to explicate a work that is too comprehensive, your analysis may touch on a little bit of everything but fail to cover anything in depth; the result will be a weak analysis. Conversely, you may discover that it is not possible to discuss one concept without analyzing the text as a whole, or to explain this text without comparing or contrasting it with another work. If your focus is *too* narrow, your analysis won't make sense. In any case, remember as you read to adjust the breadth of your questioning to the particular materials you wish to analyze.

Taking Notes

In textual analysis, you will find note-taking a valuable tool for gaining access to the author's argument. Taking notes is a personal skill which varies somewhat from student to student. You might take very detailed notes on separate note cards or simply outline the main points. Whichever method you use, check its effectiveness. For example, after you have read your text for the second time, ask yourself the questions listed above under "Reading Twice." If you cannot answer them, you may need to read the text more closely or change your note-taking technique.

In general, you should paraphrase the original text when taking notes. This means you should boil it down and put it in your own words. (See Chapter 6 for tips on effective note-taking.) You should quote only in a few special instances:

1. When the original is worded so elegantly, memorably, or powerfully that you do not want to change its effect.

2. When you just can't paraphrase it and do justice to the meaning, even though you have tried.

3. When the original is provocative or unusual, and you want to borrow the prestige of the original author to run defense for yourself, in case your reader disagrees with this point. Our own epigraphs illustrate the power of a distinguished author's exact words to enhance an argument.

When you want to use the author's exact words, be sure to mark them as a quotation on your note card so that you will properly cite the source in your paper. You must also document paraphrases (see Chapter 5).

Organizing Your Paper

Once you have read the text carefully and made notes on the most revealing passages, then you must outline your analysis and plan how to present it. The essay format is more suitable than journal format for textual analysis (see "Logic and Structure" in Chapter 1). Within the basic format there are a number of ways in which you can organize your paper. Here are three basic outline patterns you can use or modify:

Organize the body of your paper into three main parts corresponding to the three main tasks involved in explication:

1. Your explanation of what the author is saying, the author's main points.

2. Your explanation of what is behind the author's argument, for example, the polemical context or debate being addressed, the author's hidden assumptions, the author's evidence, implications of the author's points, etc.

3. Your assessment of the strengths and weaknesses of the author's argument. How well do the main points fit together? How relevant is the evidence to the points being made? How convincing are the conclusions?

Organize the body of your paper into major points which assert what you believe is most important about the text:

1. In your introduction, identify the most important features and state your position. You might also want to state the positions of other scholars unless your assignment excludes the use of outside sources.

2. In the second paragraph (or section, in a longer paper), summarize one main point you want the reader to know in order to accept your point of view and provide detailed evidence from the text to support this point.

3. Do the same thing in the third and fourth paragraphs (or sections), presenting one more major point in each.

4. In your conclusion restate your claims and summarize your points supporting them.

Organize your paper around comparing and contrasting:

There are two basic patterns you can follow to compare and contrast two works:

Pattern I	Pattern II
A (1st author)	1 (1st point)
1 (1st point)	A (1st author)
2 (2nd point)	B (2nd author)
3 (3rd point)	2 (2nd point)
B (2nd author)	A (1st author)
1 (1st point)	B (2nd author)
2 (2nd point)	3 (3rd point)
3 (3rd point)	A (1st author)
	B (2nd author)

The sample paper at the end of this chapter uses pattern II to compare and contrast Parsons' *Evolution of Society* and Marcuse's *One-Dimensional Man*. Filling in the pattern we have

1. Freedom
   A. Marcuse's assumptions about human nature.
   B. Parsons' assumptions about human nature.
2. Self-determination
   A. Marcuse's concept of self-determination.
   B. Parsons' concept of self-determination.
3. Modernity
   A. Marcuse's ideas on the relationship between modernity and the individual.
   B. Parsons' ideas on the relationship between modernity and the individual.

Writing Your Textual Analysis

Generally, your goal is to answer in writing, in a logical and coherent way, the same questions you have been asking about the text as you read. A review of the "Logic and Structure" section in Chapter 1 will help you in this task. A tip for developing a cohesive paper is to refer back to the questions you are answering as you write. They can serve as a guide in determining which information you need to make your point, and which is extraneous. Keeping your key questions in mind as you write and revise will keep you from wandering. Remember to identify the author and text in your opening paragraph.

When writing a research paper, you must follow a special set of formal conventions for documentation. For textual analysis, however, it is usually sufficient to indicate only in the first reference the publication date of the text you are using. Thereafter you may document quotations with the author's name and appropriate page number. When referring to an idea or argument found more generally throughout the text, the author's name alone, included in one of your own sentences (for example, "Parsons states . . . "), will suffice. See p. 45 for illustrations of these special citation formats. Consult your instructor for clarification and for her or his preference.

A Sample Student Paper

Since comparing and contrasting two texts is a common assignment in textual analysis, we chose a sample paper to illustrate this variation. Ellen Berlfein wrote the following paper in the spring of 1985 for a contemporary theory class. Students were told to compare and contrast any two theorists covered in the course. According to Ellen, "I emphasized Marcuse because I liked what he said. His work had a personal connection for me." Her paper compares the views of Herbert Marcuse and Talcott Parsons on freedom in modern society.

We have already outlined the variation of the essay format that Ellen appropriately chose to present her analysis. This is a slightly more complex version of the three-part essay discussed in Chapter 1. Note that she presents her thesis in the first sentence, immediately setting up the contrast. She builds her essay from there, discussing in more detail what the two theorists have in common (for example, in paragraph 1, an evolutionary view of society) and how they differ. Ellen uses the comparison-contrast mode through the entire essay to the conclusion, where she summarizes the main argument.

Since the texts are her data source, Ellen uses quotations from them to support her points. Notice, however, that the paper is not just a collection of quotations strung together. Between the quotations you will find her essay, which reflects *in her own words* what she gleaned from studying the texts. Additional comments about this textual analysis appear on pages facing the paper.

Our Comments

Here Ellen presents her thesis, answering her question "What would Marcuse think of Parsons?" But she never explicitly states this question, as she should have done clearly at the start of the paper.

In the rest of the paragraph she identifies the two theorists' different concepts of freedom, and explains the difference in terms of their assumptions about human nature. She then gives an overview of what these two positions imply for related social concepts.

In this paragraph Ellen should name the two texts she is analyzing—not just rely on the wording of the assignment to do so.

This paragraph picks up the central concept of freedom in Marcuse's text, and explains in more detail how it is connected to Marcuse's other ideas.

Ellen Berlfein
Sociology 113
Professor J. Alexander
June 4, 1985.

Marcuse and Parsons

Marcuse would accuse Parsons of being thoroughly indoctrinated by society. Although they both recognize that individuals absorb the values of their society, this fact repulses Marcuse and gratifies Parsons. Freedom is an essential goal for both theorists, but their divergent concepts of freedom reveal their different assumptions about human nature in relationship to society. Both men perceive that the structure of society has developed through a process of evolution, although not an inevitable linear progress. For Marcuse, the purpose of history is solely to welcome the final stage—when humans will be liberated from society, allowing them to unfold their true potential. Parsons doesn't consider innate, unique potential. Individuals and society evolve simultaneously, interacting and influencing each other's development. The individual is an integral part of a larger structure, acquiring his values from the society—not discovering them within himself.

Freedom in modern society is an illusion, charges Marcuse, because it is based on false needs and false values. Technological society disregards the unique values of individuals and forces them to introject the superimposed social morality.

> Introjection implies the existence of an inner dimension distinguished from and even antagonistic to the external exigencies—an individual consciousness and an individual unconsciousness apart from public opinion and behavior. The idea of "inner freedom" here has its reality: it designates the private space in which man may become and remain "himself". (10)

But our "inner freedom" has been invaded, says Marcuse. Alienated from ourselves, our minds become dominated by the values and needs imposed by society. We are naively gratified

Notice how Ellen uses the quotations from Marcuse's text to support her explication.

Notice how this paragraph matches Parson's ideas with preceding concepts from Marcuse. Ellen compares the two texts point by point, and the reader does not have the feeling that she is writing two separate papers.

This citation is ambiguous. Is the quotation about Parsons or by Parsons?

by our quantity of choices, unaware that we are really
slaves, free only to choose which master shall bind us.
"Society takes care of the need for liberation by satisfying
the needs which make servitude palatable and perhaps even
unnoticeable. . . ." (24) Marcuse cries out in indignation
toward modern society, but holds on to his faith in human
potential. Capitalism has been a necessary step, he believes,
in the evolution of history, but the final step toward
individual self-determination requires revolution rather than
evolution. Marcuse explains:

> Self determination will be real to the extent to which
> the masses have been dissolved into individuals
> liberated from all propaganda, indoctrination and
> manipulation, capable of knowing and comprehending the
> facts and of evaluating the alternatives. (252)

Parsons regards personality as an integrated system
within society. He would refute Marcuse's concept of
self-determination, claiming that an individual detached from
the hierarchical system would be like a human limb without a
brain. He believes that social evolution has been a process
of differentiation, where institutions have separated
themselves, allowing specialized systems to function
relatively autonomously. Although each system operates
somewhat independently, integration is crucial. "Identity
crises and anomie are symptoms of malintegration between
differentiated action system" (6). Contrary to Marcuse,
Parsons suggests that personal identity is formulated by
internalizing the values of the culture—lack of
internalization results in the loss of identity.

> [Parsons] conceives of a hierarchy of value guidance
> leading down from the cultural system into the society
> by way of the pattern—maintenance subsystem, then into
> the societal community, the polity, the economy, then
> out of the society into personality system, and finally
> into behavioral organism. (9)

Although the predominant value system filters downward,
influencing each level below, the subordinate systems also

Ellen refers to all people as men. Instead of "his own," she should avoid sexist language. (See Checklist for Polishing Your Paper, Chapter 10, item 13.)

This conclusion reminds the reader of Ellen's thesis, and summarizes the main positions taken in each text. The paper ends the way it began.

We like Ellen's lively, colorful, writing style, which gives us the sense that she is really personally involved with and excited by these ideas. And we encourage students to experiment with ways to express themselves and to take risks. At the same time, we would point out that an image like "smothering one's inherent jewels" does not really make much sense and might offend a reader used to a drier, more academic style.

Ellen needs to add a reference page citing complete bibliographic information about the texts she is analyzing.

influence those higher in the structure, forming an integrated cycle. Parsons admits that the norms of a society ultimately control the individual, since the individual internalizes them as his own. But rather than labeling this as false consciousness, as Marcuse would, he praises the cybernetic hierarchy because it produces a stable, efficient, adaptive society, which allows for more freedom than any previous social order. Parsons' optimistic perception of modern society is so contrary to Marcuse's because of their diverging concepts of freedom. Parsons is concerned with quantity and variability of choice, while Marcuse is concerned only with quality. Parsons argues that differentiation has provided more generalized values, allowing for the freedom of choosing previously restricted options. It has also enhanced technological advancement, which has provided material proliferation. Thus, the abundance of opportunities within industrialized society, proclaims Parsons, exemplifies our magnitude of freedom.

It is ironic how Parsons' optimistic perception of modernity stems from his pessimistic assumption about human nature, while Marcuse's pessimistic perception of modernity stems from his optimistic assumption about human nature. Parsons suggests that individuals acquire their identity from social structure, implying that they don't embody their own unique potential. Since society provides them with a personal identity, Parsons regards society as a constructive, beneficial structure. Marcuse, however, faithfully maintains that each person contains his own precious potential. He despises modern society because it smothers one's inherent jewels with false consciousness.

Chapter 8

THE ETHNOGRAPHIC FIELD RESEARCH PAPER

In an ethnographic field research project, your data come from observing or interacting with people in everyday social settings, which are known as "the field." The data are gathered through observation when a researcher visits the setting, participates in the setting's activities ("participant observation"), and/or interviews participants in the setting.

Goals and Methods of Ethnographic Field Research

1. Ethnographic field research sets out to represent as accurately as possible the process of social life *from the point of view of the participants* (or "members") in the field setting being investigated. Since a scientific hypothesis is an explanation of social processes proposed by someone *outside* the research setting, the ethnographic researcher does not engage in hypothesis-testing. In other words, ethnographic field research generally follows an *inductive* model of research (see Chapter 1).

Some sociologists engage in fieldwork as part of a *deductive* research process to test hypotheses about what happens in social settings or why. This kind of fieldwork, which we will refer to as "structured field research," is discussed in Chapter 9.

2. The ethnographic researcher usually conducts research by closely observing what people are doing, talking to them informally, and often participating in activities with them. If interviews are conducted, the ethnographer uses questions that encourage respondents to answer in their own ways and with their own words. The choice of

methods used in ethnographic research depends on the characteristics of the setting and its inhabitants and on the personal style of the researcher.

Unlike most deductive researchers, then, the ethnographic field researcher does not use a predesigned research instrument, such as a written questionnaire. And, unlike the structured fieldwork described in Chapter 9, ethnographic field research rarely involves quantitative measurement. While predesigned and quantitative methods are useful for measuring some aspects of the social world, they do not convey the intricate and subtle transactions which the ethnographer seeks to understand.

3. Reports based on ethnographic field research—called "ethnographies"—often produce new theoretical insights, but they are most distinctive for their vivid descriptions of actual social scenes and transactions. In other words, even after collecting data, the ethnographer typically does not attempt to propose a hypothesis about *why* something happens in the social world. Instead, ethnographic research attempts to uncover *what* happens in a social setting, *how* social relationships are conducted, and what those events and relationships mean to those involved.

In doing ethnographic research, your sociological imagination is exercised by the opportunity to see society's institutions, such as the police, the judicial system, or the health care system, as they are actually enacted in the personal lives of specific individuals. Because it takes sociology out of the classroom and into the "real world," and because it allows you to view the world through the eyes of people often very different from yourself, an ethnographic field research project can be especially challenging and exciting.

Asking an Appropriate Question

Often the goal of your research project will be specified by your instructor. Ethnographic research assignments frequently ask you to do one of the following:

1. Look at social interaction in your everyday life—among family, friends, fellow students, co-workers, for example—in new ways. The goals are to describe patterns and processes which often pass unnoticed in your daily interactions and to use your sociological imagination to relate these personal patterns and processes to specific course concepts. This kind of project might ask you, for instance, to talk to fellow students about their relationships with friends; observe how those in your dorm, apartment, or family deal with odd behavior; or watch how individuals attempt to present a certain impression of themselves to others.

2. Visit a setting selected by your instructor, in which social activities of special concern in your course occur, and investigate how those present carry out routine activities and make decisions. Examples of this kind of assignment are going on a police ride-along, attending traffic or small claims court, or interviewing a mental health professional.

In some classes, however, you may have to develop your own question to address through ethnographic research, or you may simply be assigned to visit a setting of your choice and describe what it is like. If so, remember that, unlike much other sociological research, the goal of ethnographic field research is not to determine what causes some social event or relationship. Therefore, avoid devising a research question that asks *why* something happens in your research setting. Instead, concentrate on asking "*what*" (for example, "What does a police officer do during his or her time on the job?") or "*how*" (for example, "How do those sharing an elevator ride deal with one another in the limited space available?"). In the sample student paper at the end of this chapter, the author addresses a "how" question: how do family members react when a relative exhibits odd or unpredictable behavior?

Here are the kinds of "what" and "how" questions that will point your ethnographic research in the right direction: What do people do in this setting? How do they explain what they do? What kinds of things interest and concern them? How do group members work together to accomplish a task? How are new members taught the values and procedures common to the setting? What do group members mean by any special words they use?

Reviewing the Literature

In a deductive research process, a review of relevant research done on the same topic is used to develop a hypothesis for testing through data collection. However, because the kind of fieldwork we are describing here does not involve hypothesis-testing, instructors assigning ethnographic research projects often do not require that you summarize the literature on the question you are investigating.

Nevertheless, your instructor, in order to encourage you to become familiar with work already done on the question you are investigating, may prefer that you give an overview of relevant research on your subject. Or you yourself may find a literature review useful in getting a feel for ethnographic research, in choosing a setting or a question for your research, or in understanding the issues of concern to those you will be observing in the field. In this case, use the guidelines in Chapter 6 to get an overview of the sociological literature relevant to your project.

Collecting Your Data

Understand the Assignment

Where are you supposed to go? What are you to look for? Are you expected mainly to present your own reactions or to describe what others do in the setting? Is the task to demonstrate your ability to apply course concepts to what you see, to provide a detailed account of interaction in the observed settings, or both? Is there a specific question you should address?

Plan Ahead

1. Begin early in the quarter or semester. Field data cannot always be collected predictably or on short notice. Furthermore, you may have to return to your field setting several times to get the additional information or understanding that you need. Your time grid (see Chapter 2) can help you allot the time you will need.

2. Make arrangements to interview or observe. While the prospect of getting permission may make you anxious at first, you will find that most people are receptive to showing you or telling you about their lives. You can assure them that their identities will remain confidential if the information is personal. Be sure to follow the procedures established by your college's Human Subjects and Ethics Committee, which might require you to submit your research plan for approval or to obtain written permission from those you observe or interview; consult your instructor for details.

When scheduling your observation or interview, allow plenty of time. Unanticipated events may occur, your subject may begin to talk at length about some particularly interesting topic, or you may think of additional questions on the spot. Also, you will need time to record, transcribe, or elaborate on notes immediately after the contact.

3. Plan how you will record your data (see the next section for a summary of recording options). In interview situations, it is best to tape record or to make notes during the interview. Likewise, notes made while observing are more reliable than those made after you've left your field setting. The methods you choose will depend on the situation and your personal style. But, whatever approach you take, be prepared ahead of time with adequate supplies of audio tape, batteries, paper, and pencil, as appropriate.

Observe the Setting

Although you may know a lot about the setting and the interactions you observe, it is crucial that you leave behind your previous assumptions and even your knowledge about them, in order to learn something new. Adopt the attitude of a naive outsider so that you can begin to look in a new way at events and experiences you used to take for granted. In other words, don't try to figure out beforehand what conclusions you should come to, or how you will use the information you are collecting. Just be as attentive to detail as you can so you can get as much valuable information as possible.

When observing: Don't presume you know which events or interactions matter most. Keep your eyes and ears open to everything that is going on around you. Notice your surroundings, all the people who are present, the time taken by events, and so on. Attempt, above all, to look at the setting or situation through the eyes of participants.

When interviewing:

1. Don't talk more than you have to. Listen carefully to the respondent.

2. Avoid leading questions which define the respondent's answer and avoid questions that point to yes or no answers.

3. Rather than asking why something happened, concentrate on asking how it occurred. "Why" questions often put people on the defensive, making them feel forced to justify their actions or life-style. Also, respondents' answers to "how" questions will be more specific about real events, providing you with the concrete examples you need to describe in detail what goes on in the setting.

4. Don't overwhelm your interviewee with multiple questions. If you are a new interviewer, you may be especially sensitive to silence, but don't rush in with comments, clarification, or further questions if the respondent pauses. Allow the respondent time to think and time to complete his or her response fully.

5. Encourage the respondent to be fairly specific about the details of events or experiences: Exactly who was involved? What happened? When did it take place? Remember, however, that probing should be gentle (for example, "Could you tell me more about that?"), not an interrogation.

6. Relax, allow your natural curiosity about your subject to direct you, and LISTEN.

Record Your Data

Since the final paper you produce will be only as good as your recorded data, it is crucial that you record observations or interview responses accurately, in detail, as soon as possible after the event. Otherwise, you will inevitably forget or distort what was said or done.

In observational research, take notes on what you see or hear as it happens. If that is impossible or bothers those you are observing, then record what you observed as soon as possible afterward. You may even want to take periodic "note-taking breaks" away from the setting during your observation to jot down a few words or phrases which will trigger your memory later.

If you are interviewing, it is best to tape the conversation. Don't be shy about asking permission to tape or take notes during the interview. People are often agreeable, once they understand your interest in accurately representing what they say.

If subjects seem reluctant to let you tape, don't force the issue. Just listen to their responses and reconstruct the interview in writing as soon as you can afterward. Don't editorialize in your reporting of what was said. Likewise, don't edit your interview to make responses seem more sensible or because something seems "inconsequential." If you edit or editorialize, you may leave out something significant. Report all the respondent's comments, keeping them in their original order. And be sure to include all your questions, as well as the answers to them.

If you do tape an interview, it will be helpful to transcribe it into written form. There are special dictation machines that make transcription easier. Or, at the least, you should listen carefully to the interview and take notes on both your questions and the responses.

In all cases, make your notes specific. Describe in detail what you observed, did, and/or heard. Like a good reporter, give the specifics of who, what, when, and where. Include concrete details about the physical setting, what went on, and your reactions: how did you feel about the people with whom you were involved? Remember that in ethnographic field research you are the research instrument; it is through your person, your interactions, and your relations that you learn about the people and settings you are studying. For that reason, your personal reactions are especially important.

You may be required to submit the originals, or a typed version, of your field notes as an appendix to your paper. Or you might choose to include your notes in an appendix, in order to give your instructor a better appreciation of what happened in your setting or interview (and of how hard you worked to gather your data!). Even if you will not be submitting your notes, keep them legible and organized. Be sure, for example, to date every entry. The quality of your paper relies on the quality of your field notes; the more clear data you have available, the stronger your paper will be.

Organizing Your Data

The observations and answers you collect in your fieldwork are the data on which your paper will be based. In this step of your research process, you use the material which you have collected to answer the question which your instructor assigned or which you formulated. This is an exciting process, because, as you look back over your notes, you will notice that the setting you have learned about in a personal way reveals interesting information about the nature of social life.

Answering an Assigned Question

If your instructor asked a specific question in your paper assignment, now is the time to consider how what you saw, heard, and experienced addresses the question. Here are some guidelines, followed by an illustration using the sample ethnographic field research paper which follows this chapter:

1. Go through your notes and make a mark by every comment, observation, or response that seems relevant to the question being asked. Don't be too discriminating at this point. Better to include too much at this stage than too little.

2. Copy these relevant pieces of data onto separate note cards, or photocopy your original notes and from the photocopy cut and paste the relevant excerpts onto the cards; this will allow you to lay the bits of data out side by side, much as you would for materials in a library research paper (see Chapter 6). Note that you should *never* cut up your original notes. Always save your original and use a photocopy or carbon for cutting. Also be sure to indicate on each card the page number of your field notes from which the excerpt was taken, so that you can include the citation if you quote the excerpt in your paper.

3. Now consider what the information on each card says in response to the question asked in the assignment. What does it tell you about the setting you observed and/or the people you interviewed?

4. Look for patterns among your cards. Move them around to illustrate to yourself how the information fits together. For instance, you might stack together cards which contain examples of the same kind of behavior. Or you might arrange appropriate cards to reflect stages in a process.

Course materials and the paper assignment itself may be useful in helping you notice the patterns in your data. Recall concepts covered in the class which are relevant to your project. Review carefully just what the assignment directs you to look at. Then consider how your data illustrate those concepts or teach you something about the social relations you observed.

For instance, Sandra Ducoff Garber, the student author of the sample ethnographic paper which follows this chapter, was asked by the instructor of her course on the sociology of mental illness to describe "the ways some particular social group . . . manage their activities so as to continue to live/work with another who is making difficulties for them." In the class, the instructor had lectured and assigned reading on various strategies which groups adopt for maintaining relationships with a troublesome member.

In analyzing her interview notes, Sandra might well have listed these strategies and then stacked in separate piles excerpts from her data which illustrated each of these strategies. Or, since she chose to tell the story of her subject's family chronologically, she might have organized her notes according to the stages which seem relevant from the subject's point of view: before age eight through junior high school; from junior high through high school; and as a young adult. With her cards ordered in these stages, Sandra could then consider how the family's definition of the problem and their response to it differed from stage to stage.

Answering a Broader Question

Perhaps you were simply assigned (or chose as your project) to participate in and describe a social setting. It will still be useful to sort out excerpts from your notes as described above, but you will probably have more freedom to establish the categories into which you will organize your observations.

Begin by carefully rereading your field notes to refresh your memory about the events. Then start to look for patterns in your notes. As in the case of an assigned question, you might use course concepts to organize this search. Better yet, you might try to find the categories and terms used by people you observed, asking yourself how *they* understand and describe their activities.

For example, if you were taking a course in deviant behavior, your text would probably spend considerable space defining "deviance" in terms of breaking social norms. But in ethnographic research you would find that the people you observe don't talk about "deviance" or "norms." Thus, rather than looking in your notes for examples of what your text would define as "deviance," it would be more enlightening to pinpoint what specific behaviors your subjects perceive as odd or disruptive and to note the ways in which they categorize and describe those who exhibit disliked behavior (such as referring to them as "weird" or as "different from us"). Similarly, a course in stratification may present sophisticated ways of measuring socioeconomic status; but, since the most interesting and valuable findings from your ethnographic field research concern the ways in which the people you observe perceive their own position in relation to society, you might look through your notes for all the ways they compare themselves to other groups.

Some of the most common themes ethnographers look for include the ways members characterize their group; the ways they distinguish between insiders and outsiders; the special language they develop to describe their shared activities and values; their patterns of interaction; the ways they teach new members the ropes; the ways they identify and respond to behavior they don't like; the ways in which members experience their setting through the course of an event, a work day, or any other unit of experience. You may find some or all of these reflected in your notes and you may find interesting themes not listed here. You may choose to focus on one area or on several related themes.

As you begin to identify themes that run through your field notes, you can proceed to sort the excerpts into piles, as described in the section above.

Writing Your Paper

Because ethnographic field research does not involve hypothesis-testing, the "essay format" discussed in Chapter 1 is more appropriate for your paper than the "journal format." Simply modify it slightly: in place of the three (or more) "claims" or "points" relevant to a paper which proposes and supports a thesis, substitute the themes or concepts which you identified in your field notes. These will serve as the body of your paper. Even though an ethnography does not always propose an answer and attempt to prove why it is more "accurate," remember that you are responsible for demonstrating, through effective use of your data, why your description of the setting is believable. Be sure to describe your research methods—where you went, how long you stayed, to whom you spoke, and so on—and to include as evidence the most illustrative excerpts from your field notes.

If the question you are addressing was assigned, you can use one of two approaches to present a written report on your observations:

First, you can describe what happened or what was said, chronologically, and comment on how course concepts apply to the things you describe, as you report them in the order in which they occurred. This is the strategy employed in the sample paper which follows this chapter.

Second, you can organize your paper around concepts, defining and indicating the importance of each, and using your data to illustrate them. In this case, you can follow the essay format, taking for each of your main points a selected concept or group of concepts.

Unless your assignment specifically requires one approach, either can be successful. If you are uncertain which approach to take, or which may be preferred, discuss your plans with your instructor. In either case, return to course concepts and themes frequently. Ask yourself how the events or comments you are describing reflect or illustrate sociological ideas. This will help you avoid the common mistake of making overly psychological interpretations of those whom you observe or interview.

If your assignment didn't specify a particular question for you to answer or a specific setting for you to analyze according to course concepts, then you can simply organize the themes you discovered in your notes into the essay format. You might choose three points to make about one of the themes that you found most interesting or revealing. Or, you might develop your paper around three different themes.

Whichever format you use, it is important for your paper to incorporate the reactions you experienced in your research and recorded in your notes. Inevitably, those engaged in ethnographic field research encounter people, events and experiences which fascinate, surprise, confuse, or even upset them. It is a challenge to make effective use of such reactions without getting sidetracked into self-analysis. A good way to make your personal reactions relevant is to ask yourself what they illuminate about the setting. Describe in your paper the ways in which your own feelings and thoughts helped you better understand the people whom you studied and their interactions.

When writing your paper, you may quote your field notes directly. When you do, punctuate and cite them as you would any other source. Or you may choose to summarize an incident or a response in an anecdotal way to illustrate a point. As long as they are relevant to your assignment, use your collected data in as many ways as you can; they make up the empirical basis for your discussion.

A Sample Student Paper

Our sample paper illustrating ethnographic field research was written by Sandra Ducoff Garber for a class in the sociology of mental illness in the fall of 1985. It responds to an assigned question: "How does some particular social group—a family, dorm hall, a living group, a work group—manage their activities so as to continue to live/work with another who is making difficulties for them?" The ethnographic method Sandra chose was to interview a woman about her family experiences. Her title, "The Purpose of Accommodation Practices in the Family: A Case Study," and her introduction alert us that she examined a family's "accommodation practices," that is, members' strategies for coping "with a father whose behavior was disruptive of the lives of the other family members" (paragraph 3). Thus the theme around which she organized the paper is drawn from the course assignment.

Sandra's essay presents this theme chronologically—how this family coped with the father at different periods in their family history. Notice that she consistently makes connections between concepts drawn from the course and empirical data collected during the interview. Her interpretations are supported by examples from her notes. Our comments on the paper point out in more detail how she has used her data to construct her paper.

Sandra's conclusion reflects her sociological imagination by showing how the interactions of one family illustrate strategies used by many social groups, including other families faced with similar challenges.

THE PURPOSE OF ACCOMMODATION PRACTICES IN THE FAMILY:
A CASE STUDY

Sandra Ducoff Garber
Sociology 157
Professor Melvin Pollner
December 6, 1985

Because of the length of Sandra's paper, she has included a title page, following the correct format (see Chapter 11).

Our Comments

Sandra's first paragraph adopts a sociological perspective by connecting her topic to social interaction and deviance.

Here she briefly reviews course materials which will be relevant to her paper.

Sandra makes it clear early in the paper how she has gone about completing the assignment: her field research consisted of interviewing an individual about how family members dealt with the father's disruptive behavior.

The introduction stimulates the reader's interest by offering a preview of some interesting findings.

The usual methods of social interaction are generally inadequate for dealing with an individual who communicates and acts in ways beyond the symbols, assumptions, and understandings of his group. As long as the group is maintained with the aberrant person as part of it, other methods must be developed.

These alternative methods of interaction have various purposes as well as forms. Edwin Lemert's "Paranoia and the Dynamics of Exclusion" (1962) studied the ways in which co-workers isolated and disempowered someone with a certain type of obnoxious behavior in the workplace. Marian Yarrow et al., in "The Psychological Meaning of Mental Illness in the Family" (1955), described the strategies of a number of wives in interpreting their husbands' odd behavior with the goal of accepting it and continuing their partnership. Michael Lynch (1983) presented and defined a large assortment of accommodation practices reported by students, mostly in coping with someone behaving oddly in their living spaces. He concluded that the accommodation practices served the group to create a "semblance of normal individuality for troublemakers" (1983:162). Presumably that semblance of normality is then extended to the groups that contain the troublemaker.

In this paper I am examining the strategies of members of a family who were trying to cope with a father whose behavior was disruptive of the lives of other family members, and who had effectively abdicated most of the responsibilities of his role as father in the family. The subject of my interview was the oldest daughter, the second child out of seven. Her description of the family dynamics indicated a very different function for the coping strategies of the children from that of their mother.

When Sally, the daughter, was eight years old, her father suffered a series of increases in financial responsibility at the same time a reorganization at his job made him very unhappy there. Three of his children became seriously ill, a purchase of some property tied up all his money, and a fifth child was born. The deterioration of his relationship with the family was gradual, but the children

Sandra could be more specific here regarding what incidents led family members to believe that their roles "had to be maintained." Also, the phrase "the implications of anyone's actual behavior" is unclear.

Here Sandra shows how the situation she is investigating illustrates concepts which have been presented in class.

Note how her interview notes are used as evidence, just as materials from a book or article might be.

Sandra accurately and appropriately applies the concept of "denial" as a way of dealing with disruptive behavior, as it was presented in the course.

were aware of their father coming home from work each night
expressing more and more anger by shouting and hissing at the
television, lecturing the children obsessively on theology
and what they felt to be inane topics, and drinking more and
more.
The parents were strictly and devoutly Catholic. The
father's authoritarian role along with the mother's
supportive and mediating role and the children's role of
obedience and unquestioning respect, all had to be maintained
regardless of the implications of anyone's actual behavior or
feelings. The members of the family did not communicate with
each other nor with anyone outside about what was going on.
The children came to avoid any communication with their
father partly as a way to "limit the gross possibility of
interaction" (Lynch, 1983:155) and partly because they found
that their ignoring him upset him.

> I did the standard trick of look [sic] at his ear and
> not at his face which just drove him up the wall and he
> would get so frustrated and so angry.

It was to the children an acceptable way to express their
anger.
By accepting her religion's concept of her role, the
mother felt absolutely prohibited from leaving the situation
or even from exerting any real pressure on her husband to
modify his behavior. Therefore, she "denied" (Yarrow et
al., 1955) her husband's outrageous behavior by refusing to
acknowledge it.

> One time my mother and sister were driving in the Loop
> and saw my father staggering drunk on a busy street in
> the Loop. And my mother said to my sister, "My God,
> it's your father! Get him in the car!" So, my sister
> pushed him into the car and my mother drove off and went
> on talking as if nothing had happened.

She was also anxious to preserve appearances and, when a
neighbor commented on the fact that the husband frequently
was heard driving away in the middle of the night, the mother
explained that "driving at night relaxed him."

Sandra uses her interview notes well. Here we can see why field research can be so rewarding, as real life examples make sociological concepts more interesting.

Here Sandra demonstrates a key point covered in class: because family life is a set of relationships from which members cannot easily escape, they must develop ways of coping with a member's disruptive behaviors.

Sandra might have commented here on the identification of the father as "sick," since the course materials focus on how those affected by troublesome behavior come to attach such a label to it.

More serious to the children were the times when she
"covered for" him (Lynch, 1983:160) regarding his behavior
toward them.

> One night he really scared me . . . I was out sleeping
> in the living room and he came up to me and he started
> saying he loved me and kissing me all over my face and
> my neck and I remember being really scared. . . . But at
> the same time, this was my dad; this was an authority
> figure; you don't push this person away. But I kind of
> did a little bit and he left very abruptly. . . . So,
> very innocently, the next day I told my mother about it
> and she got this horrible shocked look on her face and
> as soon as I saw that look on her face I realized that
> something was wrong. . . . She later told me that . . . .
> Daddy had made a mistake, that he'd thought that was her
> and not me.

If the mother did anything at that point to stop the father
from repeating such behavior, it was not effective, because
the other daughters had similar experiences with him, as
became apparent years later when one of Sally's sisters ran
away from home and another sister asked Sally if "Dad had
done anything to her."

From Sally's junior high through high school years, the
father's behavior became dramatically worse. Apparent
catalysts were the purchase of a larger home before the old
one was sold, continued growth of the family, and the entry
of the oldest children into adolescence. The children did not
feel as accepting of their father's behavior as their mother
appeared to be, but they were at least as powerless as she to
do anything overt to create any change. Exit from the
situation was still impossible for everyone in the family,
and the potential relief of communication either inside or
outside the family continued to be taboo. However, the
practices of "denial," (Yarrow et al., 1955), "avoiding
and ignoring" (Lynch, 1983:155), and various forms of
withdrawal had become inadequate.

> We knew my father was getting sick because of the way he
> was driving more and more dangerously, on the wrong side
> of the road or trying to force people off the

Sandra goes beyond rote application of course concepts by proposing fantasizing as another accommodative practice. She could make her original idea more relevant to this sociology paper by showing how the psychological process of fantasizing serves some purpose in the family's social interaction.

Here is an example of interview notes incorporated directly into the text.

"Similarly," a "sentence linker" that shows addition, functions here as a transition between paragraphs.

> road. . . . Well, we kids were terrified and sometimes
> my mother would jump out of the car. Sometimes we'd yell
> that we were scared. . . .

Thus, at a stage where turning to extrinsic remedies
would have been logical (Emerson and Messinger, 1981:173), it
was believed to be impossible, and there was no choice but to
escalate the coping practices.

All the children began to plan for the time when they
would be old enough to escape:

> The older kids planned escapes by going away to college,
> and the idea was to go as far away for as long as you
> could. I had one sister who ran away because she
> couldn't stand it.

This planning, as the subject describes it, is to some extent
fantasizing, since virtually all the children ended up going
to college at the nearest state university campus.
Fantasizing is an accommodative practice not mentioned by
Lynch (1983) or Yarrow et al. (1955).

Expressions of anger toward the father became
increasingly open. Sally, who worked in the bar where the
father drank, put up with his lewd comments in front of the
other customers. But she took great pleasure in counting her
money in front of him at home, thereby reminding him that she
had money of her own while he was deeply in debt. She paid
for many of her own expenses, including clothes, and openly
scoffed at her father when he said he'd pay her back one day.
She "went, literally, for days without speaking to the
man," and the family sat through entire meals without
speaking to one another.

One daughter became anorexic. Psychologically an
expression of self-directed anger, the anorexia also had
another, interpersonal purpose. Sally's interpretation of her
sister's behavior is that "she was going to teach Daddy how
to be disciplined." The sister was "taking over" (Lynch,
1983:158) her father's role as moral teacher, giving him her
child's role as pupil.

Similarly, Sally found herself reversing roles with her
father, "covering for" him (Lynch, 1983:60), and even

The discussion of Sally's "conflict" may be interesting but it is too psychological to be appropriate for this sociology paper.

"taking over" (Lynch, 1983:158) his responsibility as
provider in order to ensure the family's physical survival.

> My father wasn't filling out income tax forms . . . plus
> they had run out of money and they were going to
> foreclose the mortgage . . . and 'cause I was working
> then, my parents borrowed the money from me and I was
> consciously saving my money so that I could leave home
> and never come back and go away to college. . . . My
> father always made my mother do the dirty work. She was
> the one who had to ask me for the money. . . . I was
> crying the whole time. . . . I never expected to see
> that money again. . . .

Sally comments, "and I made my father feel very bad,"
obviously feeling guilty, in spite of his asking for an extra
fifty dollars which she knew was to buy alcohol. This
incident, additionally, illustrates Sally's conflict between
her acceptance of the priority of preserving the family and
her righteous anger at having to sacrifice her own goals.

The mother used her own accommodation practices so that
the family structure could be propped up, to make it appear
as if there were no trouble. One concern was appearance, not
only to people outside the family but also to those within.
This, in turn, served her main goal, which was to maintain
the power structure of the family, as she interpreted it
through her religious and cultural understanding. Through her
determination to preserve the structure of the family at all
costs, Sally's mother limited the responses the family might
make to her husband's troublesome behavior and thus
exacerbated the "organizational havoc" (Goffman, 1981) he
had initiated.

The children were permitted certain practices which
supported the power system their parents had imposed upon
them. As Lynch explains (1983), "ignoring" their father's
oddness (155), "avoiding him" as long as the "integrity of
the group" was not too severely threatened (155),
"covering" (160) and "taking over" (158) for him worked
in various ways on behalf of the family unit. These practices
and those of their mother support Lynch's conclusions about
accommodation practices, that they are "analogous, on a

This transitional sentence both refers back to the previous paragraph and introduces new material.

Here Sandra goes beyond a mechanical application of sociological concepts and demonstrates her understanding of the significance of the presence or absence of certain conditions in the family.

Conclusion clearly stated.

social level, to individual 'defense mechanisms' "
(1983:162).

However, the obligation to protect the family as a unit
in the manner insisted upon by their parents left the
children sorely in need of a way of coping with their own
resultant "alienation from place" (Cockerham, 1981:246).
They found "meaningful existence is threatened . . . mental
symptoms [and in this family, the accommodation practices
themselves] distort and destroy the very core (that is, love,
affection, respect, loyalty, responsibility) of what makes
those [family] relationships viable" (Cockerham, 1981:245).
The seven children were making great personal sacrifices to
sustain an entity that was not providing them with the
sustenance promised by its definition.

The children were unable to seek emotional support from
either inside or outside the family. They were denied the
group accommodative practices such as "humoring" the
troublemaker, sharing stories, and laughing about him, which,
as described by Lynch (1983:156,159) and Lemert (1962), might
have served to reduce his power and to "constitute a
supportive moral counterpoint" (Lynch, 1983:159).

After cooperating to protect their family, Sally's
family members were left to innovate practices as best they
could to deal with their own needs as individuals. Some of
the ways the children found to compensate for the
organizational chaos and emotional deprivation they suffered
in their family were: expressions of anger through avoiding
the father or pointedly evading his attempts at
communication; throwing up to him his decline as a provider;
withdrawing affection and respect; moral indignation;
fantasizing about leaving the family; and, finally, escaping.

In this family we see operating a complex system of
accommodative practices by nine individuals. On one level the
practices attempt to construct a desirable image for a member
who behaves in a conspicuously troublesome way; they defend
the outer integrity of the group. On another level they are a
defense by individuals in the group to prevent their own
emotional and perhaps mental destruction by the exigencies of
the social unit. The individuals may accept the priority of
those exigencies, but if the social exigencies are in
conflict with their own needs, accommodative practices must
be developed to cope with the conflict.

REFERENCES

Cockerham, William C.
1981   Sociology of Mental Disorder. Englewood Cliffs, New
        Jersey: Prentice-Hall.
Emerson, Robert and Sheldon Messinger
1981   "The micro-politics of trouble." Pp. 169-179 in
        Oscar Grusky and Melvin Pollner (eds.), The Sociology
        of Mental Illness, Basic Studies. New York: Holt,
        Rinehart, and Winston.
Goffman, Erving
1981   "The insanity of place." Pp. 179-201 in Oscar
        Grusky and Melvin Pollner (eds.), The Sociology of
        Mental Illness, Basic Studies. New York: Holt,
        Rinehart and Winston.
Lemert, Edwin
1962   "Paranoia and the dynamics of exclusion."
        Sociometry 25(1):2-20.
Lynch, Michael
1983   "Accommodation practices: vernacular treatments of
        madness." Social Problems 31(2):152-164.
Yarrow, Marion Radke, Charlotte Green Schwartz, Harriet S.
        Murphy, and Leila Calhoun Deasy
1955   "The psychological meaning of mental illness in the
        family." Journal of Social Issues 11(4):12-24.

Sandra uses the correct format for listing her references (see Chapter 4).

Chapter 9

THE QUANTITATIVE
RESEARCH PAPER

In a quantitative paper numerical data are collected to answer a sociological question. Since quantitative papers depend on specific techniques of data collection and analysis, this chapter (unlike the previous three chapters) may be most useful to students who have taken or are taking an introductory research methods course.

Most quantitative papers are based on deductive reasoning (see Chapter 1)—that is, the investigator, starting with a theory or with previous research, expects a certain answer to her or his research question. The investigator develops one or more hypotheses with the aim of predicting the results. However, some quantitative papers are based on inductive reasoning. The investigator, unsure of the answer but with some idea of what to look for, sets about to explore a particular topic. Here the purpose is description rather than prediction. No matter which approach is taken, however, the data collected can be represented numerically.

The sample quantitative paper written by Alvin Hasegawa at the end of this chapter illustrates both types of logic. Alvin uses the deductive approach in examining the relationship between student dating patterns and the prestige ranking of the student's fraternity or sorority, and he uses the inductive approach in examining the differential ranking of five date characteristics by high- and low-status "Greeks." Basing his expectation on theory and previous research, Alvin anticipated that prestige ranking would be related to dating patterns. However, his theory did not say anything specific about whether high- or low-prestige students would rate date characteristics in any particular way. Therefore he was not sure how each of the two groups would rate the five date characteristics.

This sample paper, like most quantitative papers, is written in journal rather than essay format (see the section in Chapter 1 on "Logic and Structure" for the difference between the two formats). If you are writing such a quantitative paper, divide it into the four major sections discussed below, skipping an extra line or two between sections. Capitalize and center the heading that labels each section (except for the introduction, which needs no heading). Issues that should be covered in each section include:

1. Introduction: After a review of the relevant theory and literature, what sociological question do you feel needs to be addressed? What, if any, expectations (hypotheses) do you have about the answer?
2. Methods: What method did you use in trying to answer your question? How did you select your sample? What measures did you use? What procedures did you follow?
3. Results: What patterns of numerical data did you find?
4. Discussion: What do your data mean? How do they relate to theory and/or previous research? Do the data support or refute your hypothesis?

In addition to these four major sections, other important components of your paper include the title, Abstract, References, and Appendix. These will be discussed later.

Since journal styles vary, ask your instructor which professional or scholarly journal you should use as a guide. Before starting your paper, examine recent articles from the recommended journal. (If none is recommended, use the *American Sociological Review*.) Photocopy, or carefully read through, one or two sample journal articles to use as a model of format and tone. Your paper should not only look professional but sound professional as well. Scientific communication uses a formal prose style.

Collecting and analyzing quantitative data can be time-consuming. Unanticipated problems or events may interfere with these tasks. Start early in the quarter and apportion enough time on your time grid (see Chapter 2) for these, as well as other, tasks.

We have arranged this chapter according to the steps you should follow in writing your paper. For example, although the title and the Abstract go at the beginning of your paper, you should write them during the final stages so that they describe your entire study. Therefore, we will cover these components at the end of this chapter.

The first step with a quantitative paper is to write the introduction, before collecting your data or even before selecting your method. The introduction guides your research and helps determine your focus, which is what Alvin Hasegawa discovered. When we asked him about his paper he told us: "When I write I like to start with the Introduction, to work from the beginning to end. That is different than many people who start with the body [methods section] of the paper. . . . I try to make the Introduction creative and interesting. Once I get the Introduction down, the body of the paper flows well."

The purpose of the introduction is to provide a context for the formulation and operationalization of your hypotheses. Writing the introduction involves searching and reviewing the literature, stating the problem, framing a sociological question, and, where appropriate, developing hypotheses.

Writing the Introduction

Reviewing the Literature

Once you decide on a topic, use the sources listed in Chapter 6, such as *Sociological Abstracts* or the *Social Science Citation Index*, to search for similar empirical studies of the topic. Also gather books and articles on the theory you plan to use as a framework for your study. Read and take notes as you would for a library research paper.

In writing your review of the literature, provide enough background material to place the hypothesis in its proper setting. Begin your review with a summary of the theory (or theories) from which your question is derived, specifying its major tenets and focusing on one or two aspects (or major concepts) that you would like to test. Next, discuss each relevant study, summarizing in a few sentences the theoretical approach, major hypotheses, operational definitions (measures), and conclusions drawn in each one. It is often helpful to arrange the studies in chronological order. How do these studies fit together? Do they form a pattern or are they inconsistent? Did they fail to account for an important variable? What direction did they suggest for future research?

Stating the Problem and Choosing a Question

The statement of the problem reveals the gaps or contradictory findings that you found after reviewing the chosen theory and relevant literature. Its purpose is to point out theoretical inconsistencies in need of resolution, methodological problems apparent in the empirical literature, and/or the logical next step research in this area should take. For example, you may want to concentrate on a different interpretation of a theory not adequately tested; set up a critical test of two rival theories; extend the theory to a new population or substantive area; use a new operational definition of a concept; correct the faulty methodology of a previous study; use a different design or method; or include more variables in order to look for possible interactions.

A well thought-out study which examines the relationship between two variables is better than one which examines many variables superficially. For some class assignments a simple replication of a published study may be sufficient. Be sure to check with your instructor. However, unless your study is a replication, an exact repeat of an earlier study, you must explain how your study differs from previous works, how your study will extend their findings, and what your study will contribute.

Following from the review of the literature, the statement of the problem should suggest questions that need to be answered (for example, "Is education always related to occupational attainment?"). These questions can be refined and developed into hypotheses (for example, "If ethnicity is held constant, an increase in education will be associated with an increase in occupational attainment.").

Stating Your Hypotheses

The hypothesis in a quantitative paper is the counterpart of the thesis in a library research paper. It is a formal statement expressing the relationship you expect to find between your variables. Your literature review and statement of the problem show the logic which lead to the development of your hypothesis. They serve as a sort of preliminary evidence. If your reasoning is sound, the numerical data you collect will provide further support for your hypothesis.

The hypothesis should be stated in such a way that it can be unambiguously confirmed or rejected by the results. It should also be stated in such a way as to make clear the type (causal or correlational) and direction (positive or negative) of the expected relationships. That is, does your hypothesis postulate that one variable causes the other, or does it simply state that the two variables are correlated? If the relationship is believed to be correlational rather than causal, are the variables expected to be related positively (as X increases, Y increases) or negatively (as X increases, Y decreases)? Explain how the independent and dependent variables will be operationally defined, that is, the manner in which the variables will be measured. For example, occupational attainment may be operationally defined as whether the job involves the supervision of other workers. (In correlational studies, no distinction is made between the independent and dependent variable.) Be sure to specify your unit of analysis, for example, individuals, groups, institutions, or countries.

As we stated above, if your study is purely exploratory you will not have specific hypotheses. You may simply have a question which suggested itself as an interesting problem in need of further investigation. In this case you should explain why you feel that exploring this topic is important. For some topics, a descriptive study is often an important first step leading to the formulation of a good deductive study.

Developing a Methods and Analysis Plan

Once you have drafted the introduction (except for the operational definitions of your variables) you are ready to proceed with the development of a methods and analysis plan. (Later, after you have completed the rest of your paper, you will revise and polish your introduction.) Conducting a sound investigation is crucial to writing a good quantitative paper. Therefore, it is necessary to consider in advance all the decisions you must make in collecting your data. Drawing up a methods and analysis plan will greatly improve the quality of your paper and will certainly make the writing process go more smoothly. Although it is beyond the scope of this book to discuss the multitude of methodological and statistical factors that need to be considered in conducting a good quantitative study, we do address those issues important to writing a good report of your study. These tips should be useful to both the novice and the more experienced student. However, if you are currently taking a research methods or statistics course, or have taken one or both in the past, you might want to consult your text(s) for further details.

You will be limited to certain methods depending on the kind of question you are trying to answer. For example, if you are interested in the mortality (death) rates of upper- versus lower-class men, you obviously would have to use archival sources rather than a survey. Your choice of method will also be influenced by your assignment and time and cost constraints. Below, we briefly describe the most common methods: archival sources, structured observation, experiment, and survey.

Archival sources are records of preexisting data. Although some of these data are obtained from surveys—the census, for example—we include it as archival because the results are published in tables available in government documents and books. Most of these data consist of official records of "rates," such as birth, death, marriage, divorce, crime, suicide, and accident rates. For example, you may want to examine the change in divorce rates from 1950 to 1984, the crime rates in urban versus rural areas, or the suicide rates of males versus females. To obtain these data consult a reference librarian (also see Chapter 6).

Structured field observation is different from ethnographic field research because the former is guided by set hypotheses or specific measurement objectives. Structured observation can often involve simple counting, for example, counting the occurrence of certain behaviors or the number of people in different situations. For instance, you may want to observe the frequency with which men as compared to women make supportive statements during group discussions; or count the number of students who use the coffee house for studying at different times during the day.

There are many different experimental designs, but the basic model involves two groups—an experimental and a control group. Both groups are treated exactly the same except for the independent variable(s) which is manipulated. Although we usually think of experiments as conducted in a laboratory, experiments can also be conducted in everyday settings (called field experiments). For example, you may want to examine whether people in a shopping mall will be more likely to come to the aid of a well-dressed or a shabbily dressed victim. You could manipulate the situation so that in half the cases your confederate (accomplice) comes to the mall wearing a suit, and in the other half wearing dirty jeans and a torn t-shirt.

The survey method includes both questionnaires and interviews. The logic of the survey is to replicate the experimental method artificially, although without the same degree of control, by comparing two or more groups. The groups can be based on response scores (for example, those who score high or low on a particular attitude measure) or demographic characteristics (for example, Catholics and Protestants, blacks and whites, young and old, high and low socioeconomic status). If you are interested in the different responses of males and females to a series of questions, your independent variable would be sex of respondent. In a survey, unlike an experiment, the independent variable is not manipulated. Instead, the researcher focuses on response differences that result from the naturally existing differences in the respondents.

Whichever method you choose, be sure that your proposed research is in line with the guidelines set forth by the Human Subjects and Ethics Committee on your campus (ask your instructor for details). You may need to get approval for your project from this committee.

Once you have decided on a method, draw up a plan for data collection and analysis to show your instructor. A methods and analysis plan ensures, *before you collect the data*, that your study will actually provide a test of your hypotheses. Further, it guarantees that you will be able to make sense of your data and analyze them successfully. Many students waste time and effort collecting large amounts of data only to discover later that the data do not provide a test of their hypotheses. Or, they find out that they don't know how to go about analyzing the data. A methods and analysis plan can prevent these problems.

When you write your methods and analysis plan, address those issues relevant to your type of study:

1. What population will you sample? How will you select your sample? If you are conducting a structured field study, what setting did you choose? Do you anticipate any problems in gaining access to the respondents or the field setting? How many respondents (of each type) do you need to question? How many observations do you need to make?

2. What measures will you use? That is, how will you operational-
ize your variables? How long will the questionnaire or survey take to
answer? If you plan on conducting an interview or survey, will you
use closed-ended (also known as "fixed-response") or open-ended
questions? Closed-ended questions compare to open-ended questions
as multiple choice exams compare to short-answer essay exams. What
will be the possible range of the response scale (for example, a five-
point Likert response scale) for the closed-ended questions?

If you plan to do a structured field observation, what exactly will
you look for? How long should each observation last? What things will
you want to have on your observation checklist (the list of things
which you intend to count or measure)? For example, if you want to
observe differences in how closely people of different cultures stand
next to one another, you might want to have a checklist which includes several different ethnicities and distances.

3. How long will it take to collect the data?

4. How will you get the data into an analyzable form? For example,
have you assigned an appropriate numerical equivalent (for example,
no = 1, yes = 2) to the response scales of closed-ended questions?
Have you developed a coding scheme for open-ended questions? For
example, your coding scheme could involve counting the number of
respondents who made some reference to social mobility in response
to an open-ended question, or counting the number of times different
types of respondents mentioned themes of alienation. Remember that
in a quantitative paper you must be able to represent all responses
numerically.

If you are an advanced student planning on forming an attitude
index or scale from a set of closed-ended questions, will the response
scores of any of your questions need to be reversed? That is, before
adding the response scores of several questions together to form a
single scale, will the response scores of negatively worded questions
be reversed so as to bring them in the same direction as positively
worded questions? Will you leave the index as a continuous variable
or will you divide it at the median so as to compare high and low
scorers?

5. How will you analyze the data? Depending on your hypotheses
and the level of statistical knowledge required for your assignment,
there are different ways to do this. If you haven't taken statistics, the
two simplest ways to analyze your data would be to calculate percentages or averages on each variable, independently of other variables.
Independent percentages or averages are often quite adequate for reporting the results of an exploratory study.

However, in testing hypotheses it is often necessary to look at the
relationship between two variables. The complexity of calculating
percentages or averages increases when you examine the relationship

between two variables because the variables must be examined jointly. Some common methods of doing this include constructing what is called a crosstabulation table (see Tables 1 and 2 in the sample quantitative paper), a table of means (see Table 3 in the sample quantitative paper), or a correlation matrix (not shown). In each type of table one variable is designated as the row variable and the other as the column variable.

Although constructing a correlation matrix would not be feasible, except perhaps for the most advanced student, the beginning student may be able to calculate the crosstabulation table or table of means (averages). For example, in Table 1 of the sample paper, Alvin used the prestige ranking of students' fraternities or sororities as the column variable and the prestige ranking of the dates' fraternity or sorority as the row variable.

In preparing the table, Alvin first rated the prestige level of the respondent's fraternity or sorority. Then, on the basis of this information, he sorted the questionnaires into three piles (high, medium, and low prestige). *Separately for each pile,* he counted the number of respondents who reported dating a student from a high, medium, or low prestige Greek organization. He repeated this procedure for each pile, producing a set of frequencies to be used in calculating the percentages. At the top of each column in Table 1, Alvin specified the number of students from high ($N = 10$), medium ($N = 10$), and low ($N = 10$) prestige Greek organizations. This let the reader know that the denominator used in calculating the percentages for each pile was "10." For example, he found that out of the 10 high-prestige students, 8 reported dating another high-prestige student ($8 \div 10 = 80\%$), 1 a medium-prestige student ($1 \div 10 = 10\%$), and 1 a low-prestige student ($1 \div 10 = 10\%$). At the bottom of each column, Alvin included the total percentage so that the reader would know how to read the table (for example, $80\% + 10\% + 10\% = 100\%$).

In Table 3 of the sample paper, Alvin calculated averages instead of percentages. He used student status as the row variable and the five date characteristics as the column variable. Again he designated in parentheses the number of respondents in each status category. This time Alvin sorted the questionnaires into four piles (Greek male, Independent male, Greek female, Independent female) according to the respondent's status. Then, *separately for each pile,* Alvin added together the numerical scores given by every respondent for each date characteristic. He divided each sum by the number of students in the pile. For example, the responses of the 15 Greek males in pile 1 for the date characteristic "physical attractiveness" summed to 66 ($5 + 3 + 2 + 5 + 4 + 5 + 4 + 3 + 5 + 5 + 4 + 5 + 5 + 4 + 4 + 3 = 66$). Alvin divided 66 by the number of respondents in the pile to obtain the average score ($66 \div 15 = 4.4$). Alvin repeated this procedure for each date characteristic.

Try to make a mock table for analyzing and presenting your results. That is, try to specify which variable you will use as your row variable and which variable as your column variable. Which variables will you use to sort respondents into piles? Determine whether the numbers in the cells will be percentages or averages.

If you are required to carry out more sophisticated statistical analyses of your data, determine the level of measurement of your variables (nominal, ordinal, interval, or ratio). This will allow you to decide which statistical tests can be appropriately calculated. Computer software packages that calculate social science statistics are available for microcomputers. Check with your instructor.

Don't proceed with your data collection and analysis until your instructor has approved your methods and analysis plan and answered questions. Once you complete your data collection and analysis you are ready to begin writing the other sections of your paper.

Writing the Other Sections of Your Paper

The Methods Section

The Methods section directly follows the introduction. It should contain three subparts: Sample, Measures, and Procedure. Each part should be labeled with an underlined heading at the left margin; capitalize only the first letter (see sample paper). Begin by describing your sample.

Describing your sample

Specify the population studied. Discuss in detail how you selected your sample from this population. Did you randomly select respondents, that is, give every member of the population an equal chance of being included in the sample, or did you select whomever you could get? If respondents were randomly selected, describe the steps you took to ensure randomness—for example, tossing a coin or systematically selecting every fifth residence. If you are a more advanced student, did you stratify your sample on any particular variable?

Describe all the relevant characteristics of your sample (for example, age, sex, race). If you had to eliminate any subjects because of incomplete data, or for other reasons, state the number and the reason. Specify the final overall sample size and the size of each group.

Describing your measures

If you obtained your data from secondary sources, describe where the original data came from and how they were measured. If you did a structured observation, describe the behaviors, types of people, situations, etc. that you observed.

If you used a questionnaire or interview, state whether the questions were closed-ended or open-ended, newly developed by you, or adapted from previous research. If you used existing scales or indexes, include information about their validity and reliability, if available. Validity refers to the extent to which the questions actually measure what they are supposed to measure. Reliability refers to the stability of measurements taken at different times.

In the body of the paper, quote the actual question(s) used to operationally define each variable. If several questions were used, as in the construction of an index or scale, give a sample of the questions and include the others in a table or an Appendix. For example, "Sex role attitudes were measured by agreement-disagreement with 20 statements, such as 'The woman's place is in the home' and 'I would vote for a woman presidential candidate' (see Appendix)." If the questions were closed-ended, state the range of the response scale and describe the anchor points. For example, you might state that you used a five-point Likert response scale ranging from "(1) not at all" to "(5) extremely." If you averaged several questions together to form an index, state what a high and low score on the index signifies. For example, "A high score on the sex role index indicates liberal sex role attitudes; a low score indicates conservative attitudes." If the questions were open-ended, describe the coding scheme that you used to code the data.

Describing your procedure

Identify the method you used. Describe when (time of day, day of week, date), where (the geographic location, type of institution, building), and under what circumstances the study took place. This information is especially important if the study was conducted in a field setting.

If you conducted an experiment, be sure to also specify the design. Discuss the procedure by which the independent variable(s) was manipulated and the instructions given to respondents in each group. Specify any additional precautions taken to control extraneous variables and/or exclude bias from your sample. For example, did you randomly assign respondents to experimental conditions? (Random assignment to groups is different from random selection.) If you employed confederates (accomplices), describe who they were and what they did, and whether or not they were kept "blind" (ignorant) to the hypotheses.

Whichever method you chose, summarize each step you took in collecting your data. A good rule of thumb is to describe your methods in enough detail that another researcher could replicate your study.

The Results Section

Discuss how you examined the relationship between your variables. Did you count the number of people who gave each type of response, or did you average the scores of several people? If you calculated percentages or took averages, state the number of people used as the denominator in your calculations.

If you have a large amount of data to report, consider displaying it in a table or figure. Put each table or figure on a separate page at the end of the paper, just before the References. For tables, center the table number at the top of the page with the descriptive title underneath it, so that the reader can tell what is in the table without having to refer to the text (see Table 9-1 for an example). For figures, the descriptive title goes below the graph or diagram and is left justified (starts in the farthest left column—see Figure 9-1). In the body of the paper, refer to the table or figure by number; then explain it. Remember that the numbers never speak for themselves.

If your assignment required statistical analyses, state the statistical tests performed, their critical values, degrees of freedom, significance levels, and the direction of the results. For example, "The relationship between sex role attitudes and sex of respondent is reported in Table 1. The results of a chi-square test indicate that a significantly greater proportion of females (85%) than males (55%) hold liberal sex role attitudes (χ^2 = 24.24, d.f. = 100, p < .01)." In the Discussion section, you will take this explanation a step further.

Table 9-1 Sample Table

Table 1
Sex Role Attitudes by Sex of Respondent
Sex of Respondent

		Male (N = 100)	Female (N = 100)
Sex Role	liberal	55%	85%
	traditional	45%	15%
		100%	100%

Figure 9-1 Sample Figure

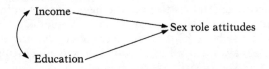

Figure 1. Measurement Model of Sex Role Attitudes

The Discussion Section

In the Discussion section you should tie your results back in to your hypotheses. Did the data support your hypotheses? Remember that the statistical significance of your findings does not indicate the theoretical, substantive, or practical significance of your findings. The latter is a judgment you must make in the Discussion section. What does a relationship between X and Y mean in the larger theoretical context? How do your findings compare with previous research? What has the study contributed to the existing body of literature on this topic? What are the practical implications of your findings, if any? What ethical issues were raised?

What is the internal and external validity of your study? That is, to what extent did your study provide an adequate test of your hypotheses? To what other populations can your findings be generalized? Discuss any methodological or design flaws, particularly if your hypotheses are not supported. Make suggestions for improving future research. If the study was methodologically sound, how can you account for your unexpected findings? Do the data support an alternative theory?

What conclusions can you draw? What direction should further research on this topic take?

The Title

Now that you've completed the main sections of your paper you will be able to come up with a good descriptive title. It should be short (rarely over 12 words), and include the theoretical perspective taken and/or the major variables examined (both independent and dependent, where appropriate). See the guidelines for Typing and Submitting Your Paper in Chapter 11.

Abstract

The Abstract, about 100–200 words, is a very brief summary of your paper. It describes the problem, method, sample, results, and conclusions of your study and should contain only ideas or information already discussed in the body of the paper. The Abstract goes on a separate (labeled) page right after the title page. For a heading, type **ABSTRACT** (all in capital letters) and center it. Triple space between the heading and the body of the Abstract. Indent the first line. Although almost always included in a journal article, an abstract may not be required by your instructor.

References

If no specific journal style is required, follow the guidelines in Chapter 4. Your References should include only those sources you actually cited in the body of your paper.

Appendix

The Appendix is optional. Some instructors may want you to include your raw data, your statistical calculations, a copy of your questionnaire, your observation checklist, your instructions to respondents, or other items. The Appendix goes after the References.

A Sample Student Paper

The following sample quantitative paper, a study of college student dating patterns, was written by Alvin Hasegawa for an undergraduate class in quantitative research methods in the spring of 1985. Choosing a date may seem like a very personal issue, but this study and others like it reveal that this individual decision is shaped by sociological factors such as class background and membership in particular organizations—for example, sororities and fraternities.

Alvin's assignment required him to work in a group with other students in designing a study, constructing measures, collecting data, and tabulating results. However, each student was responsible for writing her or his own report of the research, so this is an individual paper based on a group project. Alvin and his co-workers discussed their methods and analysis plan with the instructor before they collected their data to ensure that they were on the right track.

Alvin reviewed relevant literature on dating and developed his main thesis to answer questions raised there. The group retested other researchers' hypotheses that dating among Greek students (members of sororities and fraternities) and Independent students is homogamous, a sociological term which means that partners are chosen from within the same social group. They went beyond other studies by also asking students to rank the importance of various characteristics of a dating partner. Thus, this work is located within ongoing discussion but also contains something original—both important considerations in designing sociological research.

The paper, following a journal article format (see "Logic and Structure" in Chapter 1), is based on quantitative results from a survey. Notice that it is organized into the major sections described above: title page, Abstract, Introduction that includes a review of the literature, Method, Results, and Discussion. Alvin has also provided tables that present important results in an easily read manner. Our comments on facing pages detail additional important features of the paper as well as ways in which it could be improved.

Our Comments

Because of the length of his paper, Alvin included a title page as suggested in Chapter 11.

The title "Dating" is not very descriptive. The title should reflect the major variables being investigated. A more appropriate one would be "Homogamous Dating Among Greeks and Independents."

Dating

Alvin Hasegawa
Sociology 109
Professor Roseann Giarrusso
May 27, 1985

In the Abstract, Alvin provides a brief summary of his paper. He describes the problem, method, results, and conclusions of his study. He includes only ideas and information discussed in the body of the paper.

ABSTRACT

According to Waller (1937), dating among university
students is based on the "rating-dating complex." However,
other researchers suggest that the dating patterns of
students are more complex and may actually follow the
principle of homogamy. A survey study of university students
was conducted to examine these two theories. A total of 68
students responded to questions about the prestige ranking of
campus Greek organizations, their own dating patterns, and
the importance of five date characteristics. The responses of
male and female Greek (members of fraternities and
sororities) and Independent (non-Greek) students were
compared. The results revealed that the Greek system is
stratified on the basis of prestige and that members of the
Greek system do date in a homogamous manner. In addition, it
was found that the dating patterns of Independents also
reflect their social background. Finally, the results
revealed that Greeks and Independents differentially rank the
importance of five date characteristics. It was concluded
that student dating patterns follow the principle of
homogamy.

Alvin locates his study in the larger body of literature on marriage and the family. Also, by discussing Waller's classic study he shows that his research question is rooted in a long-standing sociological tradition.

As suggested in Chapter 10, Alvin uses the phrase "in contrast" as a transition between paragraphs.

Here, Alvin shows how the positions of Reiss and Krain et al. differ from Waller's. These studies try to show the limitations of Waller's earlier work. Alvin briefly refers to the theory, hypotheses, methods, and results of these two studies.

Most of us hope that someday we will find that perfect someone whom we will marry. But, in order to accomplish this task, we must go through that courtship system commonly known as the marriage market. Thus, in order to select a mate, we must first go through the dating process. Our group study focused on this aspect of marriage and the family.

In our search for existing data, we came across two important studies. The first was done by Reiss (1965); the second, by Krain, Cannon, and Bagford (1977). Both studies were based upon earlier work done by Waller (1937) on the "rating–dating complex" on college campuses. According to Waller, casual dating among Greeks (members of fraternities and sororities) is a prestige contest based mainly on factors such as having a car, money, and nice clothes, and belonging to the best fraternity/sororitiy. However, this status–seeking pattern isn't true for seriously dating couples whose goal is mate selection.

Reiss (1965), in contrast to Waller, hypothesized that the Greek class system and related dating actually reflects parental class background. This pattern of dating supports the principle of homogamy because it encourages marriage among those who are similar in social background. To test this hypothesis, Reiss used two surveys: one to rank the Greek organizations and a second to obtain information on Greek dating patterns. He found that most of those in high–ranking Greek organizations had fathers in high occupations (executives, etc.). This was less true in the low–ranking Greek organizations. In the second part of his study, he found that high–ranking Greeks tended to date other high–ranking Greeks, whereas low–ranking Greeks dated elsewhere. This finding supported his hypothesis and showed how parents unintentionally achieve homogamy.

Krain et al. (1977) hypothesized that "stratified prestige structures [do] exist to differentiate Greek organizations from each other" (666). They also believed that dating would tend to be confined within the levels of such structures. Unlike Waller, however, they assumed that serious as well as casual dating would reflect prestige homogamy. With this, they developed two surveys: one on perceptions of Greek organizations' prestige and a second on dating patterns among those with Greek affiliation. They

A review of three studies is not "thorough." Alvin should either acknowledge that the review was very selective or state that there were few studies conducted on this topic (which, in this case, is not true).

Here, Alvin states three hypotheses, clearly and in a way that can be unambiguously confirmed or rejected.

Here he introduces some new questions.

Replication means more than just using the same method. Alvin should have specified exactly how his study is the same.

How many of each group? How many of each sex? What age range?

Alvin included the questionnaires in an Appendix (not included in this book, however, for the sake of brevity).

found support for both of their hypotheses in the analysis of
their results.

    After a thorough review of the literature, we decided to
retest the hypotheses formulated by these earlier
researchers. Our first two hypotheses dealt with the Greek
system here at UCLA. Based on Krain et al.'s (1977) study,
our first hypothesis was that Greek systems will be
stratified in terms of hierarchical prestige ratings. Our
second hypothesis was that those in the Greek system will
tend to date in a homogamous manner based on the prestige
ranking of their Greek organizations. Our third hypothesis
tied in with Reiss's (1965) work, but instead of dealing with
Greeks, it concerned "Independents"—non-Greek UCLA
students. Thus, our third hypothesis was that parental class
background will be reflected in the dating patterns of
Independents. Finally, we decided to ask some questions not
included in either of the above studies on the rank-order
importance of five characteristics in a dating partner. Since
we did not have any hypotheses about these characteristics,
these questions were just exploratory.

                          METHOD

Design
    Because we chose to use hypotheses previously tested, we
simply replicated the research design, i.e., we used the
survey method.

Respondents
    We surveyed a total of 68 students from two separate
groups: Greeks and Independents.

Measures
    We constructed two different survey instruments (see
Appendix). The first would be used to place the Greek
organizations into ranks, according to prestige. The second
survey would be used to measure, for both Greeks and
Independents, demographic information, dating patterns, and
the rank-order importance of five characteristics in a dating
partner.

The word "data" is plural, not singular. Therefore, the verb should be plural: "The data were . . ."

Anyone? How were the subjects selected? This section is very weak. Alvin should have given enough detail for another researcher to replicate his study.

Here Alvin tries to control for bias in the data analysis.

Where are the data? He should have included them in a table.

Alvin refers the reader to the table, then explains what the numbers in the table mean.

Procedure
       After completing the surveys the next step was to
collect the data. The data was collected over the weekend of
April 21, 1985. The first survey, which asked students to
rank-order the various Greek houses on campus, was given to
anyone who had knowledge about the fraternities and
sororities. This survey was given to 15 Greek individuals.
Our second survey, measuring dating patterns and the
importance of the five characteristics, was administered to
both Greeks and Independents. This survey was given to 30
Greeks (15 males and 15 females) and 23 Independents (15
males and 8 females). The Greek participants were surveyed at
their respective houses, while the Independents were surveyed
at the dormitories.

RESULTS

       In analyzing our first survey, student rankings of
his/her own organization were excluded from the results in
order to control for partiality toward one's own Greek
organization. We found that the Greek system was indeed
stratified, as our data showed a clear-cut view of the
separate classes. Each house fell neatly into one of three
categories: high, medium, or low. There seemed to be a
consensus as to which houses were at the top and which were
not.
       Our second survey on homogamous dating patterns had to
be analyzed separately for Greeks and Independents, owing to
the different criteria on which prestige was based for each
group.
       In our analysis of Greeks, we used the results of the
first survey to divide students (based on their Greek
membership) into high, medium, or low prestige. Of the 30
Greeks surveyed, an equal number of males and females (5
each) came from high, medium, and low-ranking fraternities
and sororities. The results are reported in Table 1. We found
that Greeks in the high-prestige organizations tended to date
other high-prestige Greeks. Those Greeks in the medium-
prestige range dated both within their own category and with

Unless your instructor says otherwise, each table should go on a separate page at the end of your paper, just before the References, rather than in the body of the paper.

Very good table. In order to test his hypothesis, Alvin crosstabulates two nominal level variables to examine their relationship.

Where are the data on sex differences? Again, he should have included these in a table.

Alvin details exactly how social class was calculated and refers to the source of this formula.

The cutoff point used to divide subjects into categories is specified.

It was a good decision to analyze the data separately for males and females, since the females were all upper class.

Table 1.

Prestige Ranking of Member's Greek Organization by Prestige
Ranking of Date's Greek Organization

Prestige of Member's Greek Organization

		H (N = 10)	M (N = 10)	L (N = 10)
Prestige of	High	80%	40%	10%
Date's Greek	Medium	10	50	20
Organization	Low	10	10	70
	Total	100	100	100

those in higher categories. For those in the low-prestige
organizations, our results showed that they dated within
their own category. These findings were characteristic of
both males and females in the Greek system. We also noted
that women in high-prestige categories did not date any less
prestigious Greeks, and the low-prestige men did not date any
higher-ranked Greeks.

Next, we had to analyze the data from our Independent
subjects. In order to get prestige rankings for students in
this group, we used a measure that reflected parental class
background. There were two questions on the survey which
inquired about their father's occupation and education. Using
this information and a social class rating formula, we could
determine social class ratings. The formula was:

(Occupational Rating × 7) + (Educational Rating × 4) =
Social Class Rating.
(See King and Ziegler 1975, for a description of this
formula.) We decided that any score of 60 and above would
rank in the upper-class/high-prestige category. Anything
below 60 would fall into the lower-class/low-prestige
category.

Of the eight female Independents, none fell into the
lower- or middle-class category. However, in classifying the
male Independents, we were able to separate them into upper
and lower classes. Therefore, we decided to analyze the
results separately for male and female Independents.

Again, nice presentation of the results. The column and row variables of the table are clearly labeled and a descriptive title is provided. For each row, the size of each group is specified in parentheses and the total percent is included so the reader will know how the table should be read.

This type of statement relating the size of the group to the conclusions should go in the Discussion section, not the Results.

Subjects may have found the response categories 1 to 5 confusing since they were asked to rank (rather than rate) each characteristic.

Table 2.

Prestige Ranking of Independent Females and Males by Prestige
of Date

Prestige Ranking of Independents	Prestige of Date			
	Greeks	Independent/ Off-Campus	Don't Date	Total
Upper Class Females (N = 8)	25%	50%	25%	100%
Upper Class Males (N = 9)	56	33	11	100
Lower Class Males (N = 6)	0	50	56	100

Table 2 shows that 50 percent of the female Independents
date Independent or off-campus males, i.e, nonstudents,
although our hypothesis would have predicted a similar number
dating Greeks (since the females are of high social class).
However, because of the very small sample size, these results
are inconclusive.

We also see from Table 2 that a large number of male
Independents date both Greek and Independent females in the
upper-class category. In the lower class, note that none of
the Independent males date Greek females, and half of them do
not date at all.

Finally, we analyzed the results of the rank ordering of
the five characteristics in a dating partner. We did the
analysis separately for males and females, Greeks and
Independents. Subjects ranked each characteristic on a
five-point scale from "(1) not at all important" to "(5)
extremely important." In Table 3 we show the average ranking
of each characteristic, for each subgroup. We can see that
the scores for all five characteristics for females, whether
Greek or not, are the same. Both Greek and Independent
females ranked personality as most important, and potential
occupational success as second most important. For the males,
the results are quite different depending on their Greek
affiliation. Greek males rated physical attractiveness as the
most important characteristic, whereas the Independent males

Alvin constructs a table of means to determine whether any differences exist between males and females or Greeks and Independents in terms of the importance of various characteristics of a date.

Again, the verb should be "were," not "was."

In the Discussion section, Alvin reintroduces his hypotheses and states whether they were supported.

Table 3.
Average Rankings of Five Characteristics by Male and Female
Greeks and Independents

	Physical Attract- iveness	Person- ality	Sense of Humor	Potential Occupational Success	Attitude Similarity
Greek Males (N = 15)	4.4	3.8	2.9	1.4	2.4
Independent Males (N = 17)	2.6	3.8	2.9	1.3	2.4
Greek Females (N = 15)	2.8	4.2	2.5	3.1	2.3
Independent Females (N = 8)	2.4	3.3	1.9	2.5	2.0

thought personality was the most important. Physical
attractiveness came in third, after a sense of humor, for
male Independents.

DISCUSSION

Now that all the data was analyzed, we reviewed our
hypotheses. Our first hypothesis, that the Greek system would
be stratified according to prestige, was supported by our
first survey. It showed a consensus of opinion about which
houses belong to high-, medium-, or low-prestige categories.
Our second hypothesis stated that Greeks would tend to date
in a homogamous manner. This, too, was supported. We saw, in
general, that high-prestige Greeks date other high-prestige
Greeks. The Greeks in low-prestige categories also date each
other.

The fact that the medium-prestige Greeks dated both high
and medium Greeks may at first be deceptive. But it too
supports our second hypothesis. Those who dated from medium

Here Alvin offers an interpretation of the results. He introduces the concept of self-esteem and shows how this concept can explain his findings.

This effective transitional sentence reminds the reader what the paper has already addressed and summarizes what's coming next (although all transitional sentences do not have to follow this pattern).

Alvin went beyond replication by bringing in a new set of questions. However, he should have gone further in interpreting the findings.

Here Alvin makes a concluding statement. He relates his findings to previous research and notes the contribution of his study.

Although this paragraph highlights the importance of managing your time, it is irrelevant to Alvin's discussion of his study's weaknesses. Alvin's critique should be directed toward the limitations of his methodology.

to high may have had high self-esteem and perceived themselves as dating a Greek of similar status.

Our third hypothesis was that the dating patterns of Independents would reflect their social class background. Since we assumed that Greek organizations have prestige, we expected to find that upper-class Independents would date as many Greeks as Independents, and that lower-class Independents would stay away from Greeks. Our results seem to have confirmed this hypothesis. We found that upper-class Independents were able to date Greeks just as frequently as they did Independents. And we found that the lower-class Independents did not date Greeks at all; they stayed with the Independents or did not date.

In addition to the three hypotheses we tested for, we had subjects rank five characteristics of a date in order of their importance. Although we had no clear hypotheses as to what we could expect, the results were interesting. It is interesting to note, for example, that "potential occupational success" was ranked second in importance by all females. This may imply a female's need for security and a belief in the traditional role of male support. The results for the males were influenced by Greek affiliation. Although Independent males' ranking of the importance of physical attractiveness was similar to the females, the Greek males rated it as the most important characteristic. Are Greek guys really only interested in a girl's body?

All in all, our results seem to have supported our hypotheses, and the data has been consistent with previous findings. Although our research model paralleled others, our study did add to the previous studies by applying earlier concepts to a new sample, and by comparing how Greek and Independent males and females rank order the importance of characteristics in a date. However, this is not to imply that there were no problems with our research. Nothing could be less true.

Time is a limited resource, and for our group, it was very precious. Although we had ideas in our head as much as three weeks in advance, it wasn't until a week before our presentation that we got them down on paper. That, perhaps, was our major downfall, but not our only one.

The survey itself was not perfect. It contained oddly

Alvin should have put quotation marks around the words "casual" and "serious" to indicate to the reader that these were the actual words used in the questionnaire.

This is a common mistake made by students. In scientific communication, "random" means something more than what we mean in everyday language. Alvin also seems to have misunderstood that it is the selection process, not the sample size, that determines the representativeness of the sample.

It is important to be aware of any ethical problems with your study before you undertake data collection. Alvin shows that he was sensitive to this issue.

At the polishing stage, Alvin should have revised to avoid four "he or she" phrases in close proximity. See checklist in Chapter 10 for further explanation.

Unless your assignment requires some discussion of the group processes experienced while undertaking your research project, this type of information should not be included. Also, the informality of the last sentence is inappropriate for scientific communication.

Alvin should have ended his paper by suggesting a direction for future research.

worded questions and vague ideas. A few questions could have
been reworded in order to prevent confusion. In particular,
we might have operationally defined some terms such as casual
or serious dates. Finally, our last question should have read
"rate" instead of "rank." This minor detail could have
made a major difference in our results.

Another problem related to the survey was our sample
population. With only 68 subjects in all, our results could
not have been highly representative. And, although our
subjects were chosen at random, it was not completely random.
Since we sampled residents of only one floor of the dorm, the
results may only reflect the attitudes of students on that
floor and not the entire UCLA population.

As far as ethics are concerned, this research was pretty
fair. Our surveys were anonymous, so no one would feel as if
they are giving up intimate secrets for everyone to see. The
only ethical issue that might arise would be if a subject
discovered that he or she was in a low-prestige ranking or if
he or she found out that he or she did not date. Of course,
the subject knows whether he or she dates, but the survey may
rub it in. The realization that one does not date may result
in lowering self-esteem.

In conclusion, our group made up for our problems with
our effort. Although, we could have (and should have) started
earlier, we didn't. But, that didn't stop us. We all worked
hard, and with cooperation, we finished our project fairly
successfully. Now that we're through, we can all relax, and
go out and find some dates.

REFERENCES

King, Michael, and Michael Ziegler
  1975 Research Projects in Social Psychology: An
        Introduction to Methods. Monterey, Calif.:
        Brooks/Cole Publishing Co.

Krain, Mark, Drew Cannon, and Jeffery Bagford
  1977 "Rating–dating or simply prestige homogamy."
        Journal of Marriage and the Family 39:663–674.

Reiss, Ira L.
  1965 "Social class and campus dating." Social Problems
        13(2): 193–205.

Waller, Willard
  1937 "The rating–dating complex." American Sociological
        Review 2:727–735.

Alvin includes in his Reference section only the sources he actually cited. Also, he follows the format recommended in Chapter 4.

PART III

FINISHING UP

It has long been an axiom of mine that the little things are infinitely the most important.

SHERLOCK HOLMES IN CONAN DOYLE'S
"The Adventure of the Copper Beeches"

Chapters 10 and 11 of this book will help you complete the paper-writing process. Although we encourage you to read this section before you begin your paper, it will be especially helpful after you have typed your second draft and before you type the final copy.

Chapter 10 tells you how to fine-tune. After you type your second draft, get away from it—for several days if possible, for a good night's sleep at least. Efficiency in spotting weaknesses increases dramatically with distance from the paper, and flaws that escape your bleary eyes at 2:00 A.M. often leap off the page when you are rested.

At the fine-tuning stage, the most difficult parts of the writing process are behind you. In fact, some writers who do anything "to avoid writing the first word" (see the quotation at the beginning of Chapter 2) actually *enjoy* polishing. Think of polishing as a way of showing hospitality, and your reader as a special guest whom you would not dream of putting to work. For example, bring a fuzzy argument into sharp focus; at points where you have moved abruptly from one point to another, supply transitions, connecting the components of your argument for your reader; and correct punctuation, citation errors, and spelling so as not to confuse or distract.

How important is punctuation? And why does the very word often provoke negative feelings? Rudolf Flesch comments in *The Art of Plain*

Talk: "Punctuation, to most people, is a set of arbitrary and rather silly rules you find in printers' style books and in the back pages of school grammars. Few people realize that it is the most important single device for making things easier to read" (Flesch, 1962:108). But negative feelings also arise from lack of confidence in manipulating punctuation (and other matters of style, such as sentence structure). Style manuals (mentioned in Chapter 3) can help, but if you enjoy learning from people more than learning from reference books, investigate writing courses at your college. Some colleges attach adjunct writing courses to sociology and other courses.

Chapter 11 supplies guidelines for a step in the writing process that really matters, the presentation of your paper. In some cases, your paper will be among dozens that your probably overworked instructor must evaluate. Imagine your own irritation if, after reading students' papers for hours, you picked up one that was typed with a faint typewriter ribbon that should have been replaced long ago; or, conversely, imagine your sigh of relief and gratitude when the next paper in the stack is easy to read. Although a nicely presented paper that lacks substance will not likely fool even the weariest instructor, studies reveal that a professional-looking paper implies a smart and serious student and often contributes to a better grade. Taking the time to "package" a carefully written paper also shows respect for your instructor's workload—a respect he or she may well be inclined to return.

At this stage you are on the last lap, but do not underestimate the importance of a strong finish. Therefore, allow ample time for careful—not rushed—polishing, typing, and proofreading. Following the suggestions in our last two chapters can turn "poor" into "satisfactory," "good" into "excellent."

CHECKLIST FOR POLISHING YOUR PAPER

1. Can you quickly identify your thesis—that is, your central argument?

2. Does your thesis remain evident and central throughout the paper?

3. Do you support your thesis with adequate evidence? One trick for checking the quantity and quality of your evidence is to put a mark in the margin of a rough draft wherever you see evidence for your thesis, pausing at each point to review its validity. Instructors sometimes use this method when evaluating the soundness of an argument.

4. Is there a clear, logical relationship among all the paragraphs? If one is irrelevant to your thesis—no matter how dazzling—delete it; if one wanders from the topic, bring it back into line. Stick to the subject.

5. Repeat 4 (above), substituting "sentences" for "paragraphs."

6. Does the writing flow back and forth between generalizations and specifics that support and clarify those generalizations?

7. Are there transitions between paragraphs? Sometimes transitions seem to create themselves naturally during the writing process. Other times you have to create them, very deliberately, at the polishing stage. But make them look natural, not slapped on. The smoothest transitions, perhaps, come in the first sentence of each paragraph, deftly referring back from where you came and forward to where you are going. However, the sample student paper in Chapter 1 includes an example of a transition that occurs at the end of a paragraph. Your reader will be grateful for transitions because the ride through the paper will be smooth, not bumpy.

8. Now pay attention to transitions between sentences. Sometimes the logical connection between sentences is clear without adding any-

thing. However, there are some common words and phrases for maneuvering between sentences, sometimes called "sentence linkers," that you already use, probably unconsciously, in your writing and daily conversation. Consider inserting a few of the following sentence linkers, using appropriate ones. If you use ones you do not fully understand, you might diminish rather than enhance the quality of your paper.

To show addition: again, also, and, and then, besides, equally important, further, futhermore, moreover, next, similarly, too, what's more.

To show time: after, afterward, as, at length, at once, at the same time, by, earlier, eventually, finally, first, formerly, gradually, immediately, later, next, once, previously, second, soon, then, thereafter, while.

To make the reader stop and compare: after all, although, at the same time, but, conversely, for all that, however, in contrast, in the meantime, meanwhile, nevertheless, nonetheless, notwithstanding, on the contrary, on the other hand, still, whereas, yet.

To give examples: as an illustration, for example, for instance, in other words, to illustrate, to demonstrate.

To emphasize: as a matter of fact, clearly, in any case, in any event, in fact, indeed, more important(ly), obviously, of course, that is.

To repeat: as I have said (demonstrated, argued, noted, etc.), in brief, in other words, in short.

To draw a conclusion: accordingly, as a result, at last, consequently, hence, in brief, in conclusion, in sum, on the whole, so, therefore, thus, to conclude.

9. Do all your words mean what you think they mean? For those occasional moments of doubt, we recommend your owning a good hardcover dictionary (the College Edition of *The American Heritage Dictionary of the English Language* is one good choice) as well as a portable paperback if you sometimes write and study in the library. As we mentioned in Chapter 3, be especially careful when using terms that have become part of everyday language and yet retain special sociological definitions (the examples we gave were "stereotype," "status," and "self-fulfilling prophecy"). If you're uncertain about the sociological definitions of your key terms, you might find them quickly in sociology textbooks by using the index and/or glossary. Several dictionaries of sociological terms are also available.

When dealing with words that do not have special sociological meanings, a thesaurus can help you both to locate the most precise word that expresses what you want to say and to find synonyms for varying your word choice. The popular paperback *Roget's College Thesaurus*, in dictionary form, is simple to use because words are alphabetized just as they are in a dictionary. However, before you use a synonym from a thesaurus in your paper, check its meaning in a dictionary. Mark Twain said that "the difference between the almost right word and the right word is really a large matter—'tis the difference between the lightning-bug and the lightning." Believe it or not, the search for "just the right word" can be fun.

10. Have you looked carefully for errors in style (sentence structure, punctuation, spelling, citation)? As we mentioned in Chapter 3, reference books which present style guidelines are available in most bookstores and libraries. Now, at the polishing stage, it may be valuable to consult such a source. *The Chicago Manual of Style* and Kate L. Turabian's *A Manual for Writers of Term Papers, Dissertations, and Theses* are reputable manuals, but your instructor may recommend another. See Chapter 4 for one citation format used widely in sociology.

11. What about contractions (for example—it's, don't, you're)? If occasionally or consistently using contractions feels more natural to you than writing the words out (it is, do not, you are), then ask if your instructor objects. If you have waited until the last minute and do not know your instructor's preference—which may vary according to the assignment—then play it safe and avoid contractions (for example, they are not appropriate for the journal format).

12. Have you stated your conclusion clearly and forcefully?

13. Have you inadvertently used sexist language (for example, used the masculine pronoun "he" exclusively)? Many writers would prefer to use nonsexist language, but repeating "he or she" (or "she or he") every time a singular pronoun is required can sound awkward and repetitive. An occasional "he or she" sounds fine; but two in one sentence or, say, three in one paragraph are distracting. Sometimes writers "solve" this problem but create another by following a singular noun or pronoun with the non-gender-specific, but plural, pronouns "they" and "their." For example, here is a paragraph from Alvin Hasegawa's paper in Chapter 9:

> As far as ethics are concerned, this research was pretty fair. Our surveys were anonymous, so no one would feel as if they are giving up intimate secrets for everyone to see. The only ethical issue that might arise would be if a subject discovered that he or she was in a low-prestige ranking or if he or she found out that he or she did not date. Of course, the subject knows whether he or she dates, but the survey may rub it in. The realization that one does not date may result in lowering self-esteem.

In what looks like an admirable attempt to write in a nonsexist manner, Alvin erroneously changes a singular pronoun to a plural one ("so no one would feel as though they . . .") and then uses four *he or she's* in close proximity. In many cases you can easily manipulate language so that it is both nonsexist and grammatically correct by using plural subjects, which can be followed, quite correctly, with "they" or "their." Here is one possible revision of Alvin's paragraph:

> Ethically, this research was pretty fair. Our surveys were anonymous, so respondents would not feel as if they were giving up intimate secrets for everyone to see. The only ethical issue that might arise would be some subjects' discovering that they were in a low-prestige ranking, or if they found out that they did not date. Of course, the subjects know whether they date or not, but the survey may rub it in, resulting in lowered self-esteem for some respondents.

In changing from a singular to a plural subject, however, be careful that you do not change the meaning or emphasis of the sentence.

Example (from Ellen Berlfein's paper, Chapter 7):

Before: The individual is an integral part of a larger structure, acquiring his values from the society—not discovering them within himself.

(A possible) after: Individuals are an integral part of a larger structure, acquiring their values from the society—not discovering them within themselves.

If Ellen wants to emphasize the singularity of the individual, however, a plural subject might not be appropriate, and she would have to experiment with other possible revisions. One possibility:

> The individual is an integral part of a larger structure, acquiring his or her values from the society—not discovering them internally.

Chapter 11

TYPING AND SUBMITTING YOUR PAPER

Find out your instructor's preferences, if any, about format, including title page, citation, and appendix(es), if applicable. Unless your instructor specifies otherwise, follow these fairly standard guidelines for typing and submitting your paper:

1. Use a reasonably new typewriter or printer ribbon. Clean your typewriter keys, if necessary. You do not want the instructor remembering your paper as the one with annoyingly faint print or the one with all the *e's* and *o's* filled in.

2. Type on sturdy white paper (not onionskin or erasable). Leave margins of one to one-and-one-half inches on all sides.

3. Double-space throughout the text of the paper, except for quotations longer than five lines, which should be single-spaced and indented five spaces from the left margin. (Do not indent the right-hand margin.)

4. A quick review of Chapter 4 will remind you of the proper form for citing sources in the text of your paper and for "References" or "Bibliography," a list which follows the text.

5. Depending on the type of paper you've written, some instructors may want you to include your raw data, statistical calculations, a copy of your questionnaire, observation checklist, instructions to respondents, ethnographic field notes, or other items. As appropriate, you should make each of these items an appendix to your paper. (*The American Heritage Dictionary* defines "appendix" as "supplementary material.") The appendix belongs after the References or Bibliography on a separate, titled page. If your paper requires more than one appendix, number or letter each one (Appendix 1, Appendix 2, etc. or Appendix A, Appendix B, etc.). Number pages of the appendix(es) as if

they were additional pages of the text—if, for example, the last page of the text is numbered 5, the first page of the appendix would be 6.

How you should space an appendix (single, double, etc.) depends on the nature of the material and how it can most easily be read; spacing need not be the same for all appendixes. However, the heading will ordinarily be centered and triple-spaced—that is, you triple-space between "Appendix" and the title and triple-space again between the title and the body of the appendix.

6. After typing the final copy of your paper, proofread, proofread again, and have someone proofread for you. Look for errors in punctuation and spelling, typos, and omissions. Some sentence-structure problems can be easily fixed, even on the final copy. For example, a sentence fragment might be made into a complete sentence by inserting a word or two, although generally it is not acceptable to insert more than a few words by hand.

If you are working with a computer, you might choose to make your corrections at the keyboard and then print out another copy, depending on the number of the corrections and their complexity. Using a typewriter, however, is another matter: another copy is not so easy to make, and, despite your best efforts, you may need to make some corrections on the copy you turn in. Correction fluid (for example, Liquid Paper) and correction tape are some of the products available for making "clean" corrections at the typewriter. However, some corrections may have to be made in ink.

Here are some of the most common corrections, which can be made in ink by using conventional proofreaders' marks. You may want to combine some of these commonly understood proofreaders' marks with your favorite correction method; for example, you may prefer to use correction fluid to white out a misspelled word rather than strike it out as is suggested below. Most instructors are more concerned with the end—corrections that are instantly intelligible—than the means.

To insert, put a caret ($_\wedge$) just below the line at the place where you want to insert and then write in the word or phrase directly above the caret.

Example: This is what you do if you have left_out_a word or phrase.

To delete, put a single line through the word or phrase.

Example: the ~~good~~ word

If you omitted a space while typing, draw a vertical line between the words you want to separate.

Example: the|word

If your typewriter has skipped a space in the typing of a word, close the space with a pair of horizontal parentheses.

Example: typ͡ing

If letters need transposing, do this:

Example: t͡h̷typing

If you have badly misspelled a word, draw a single line through it and write the correction directly above it. If you have omitted only one letter, insert it by using a caret.

Example: accomo͡date

If you have failed to indent a paragraph, put the paragraph sign (¶) right before it.

7. If you use a title page, center your title horizontally and place it halfway down the page. In the lower right-hand corner type your name, the course number (for example, Sociology 101), the name of your instructor, and the date. Number pages beginning with the first page of the text, not with the title page. Sometimes instructors do not require a title page for short papers (approximately five or fewer pages). If you're not using a title page, provide the same information (your name, the course number, the instructor's name, and the date) in the upper right-hand corner of page 1; triple space and center the title; and triple space again before you begin the first paragraph.

8. Fasten the paper with one staple, not a paper clip. Do not use a cover or folder, which creates unnecessary bulk for your instructor's briefcase and unnecessary expense for you.

9. Keep a photocopy of your paper to insure against loss or misunderstanding.

REFERENCES

Durkheim, Emile
[1897] Suicide. Glencoe, IL: Free Press.
1951

Flesch, Rudolf
1951 The Art of Plain Talk. London: Collier.

Fowler, Henry W.
1965 A Dictionary of Modern English Usage. 2nd edition. Ernest Jawer, ed. New York: Oxford University Press.

Galbraith, John Kenneth
1978 "Writing, Typing, and Economics." Atlantic Monthly. March: 102–105.

Lanham, Richard
1979 Revising Prose. New York: Scribner's.

Mills, C. Wright
1959 The Sociological Imagination. New York: Oxford University Press.

Olson, Gene
1972 Sweet Agony. Grants Pass, OR: Windyridge Press.

Plimpton, George (ed.)
1965 Writers at Work: The "Paris Review" Interviews. Second Series. New York: Viking.

Stark, Rodney
1985 Sociology. Belmont, CA: Wadsworth.

Turabian, Kate L.
1973 A Manual for Writers of Term Papers, Theses, and Dissertations. 4th edition. Chicago: University of Chicago Press.

University of Chicago Press
1982 The Chicago Manual of Style. Chicago: University of Chicago Press.

ABOUT THE AUTHORS

The eight members of the Sociology Writing Group came together in 1984 to prepare a guide for instructors and students in sociology and writing courses at UCLA. *A Guide to Writing Sociology Papers* grew out of this collaborative effort. Although each member had major responsibility for some particular contribution to the project and also worked on other specific parts, all read and commented on one another's work. Judith Richlin-Klonsky and Ellen Strenski coordinated the group's work and edited the book.

Constance Coiner received her M.A. in English from UCLA and is completing an interdisciplinary Ph.D. program in English and history. She has taught UCLA composition courses for four years and received the UCLA Faculty Prize for Distinguished Teaching Assistants. Ms. Coiner is a Woodrow Wilson Fellow and was awarded the UCLA Distinguished Scholar Award. She co-authored *Writing Historical Essays* (published by UCLA) and is a contributing editor to *Reconstructing American Literature* (forthcoming). Constance Coiner contributed major portions to Chapters 2 and 3 and contributed to Chapters 4 and 5. Part III is her work. She also helped edit the book.

Arlene Dallalfar received her M.A. in sociology from UCLA. She has been a teaching assistant in diverse courses ranging from social theory to mental health and has been the consultant to teaching assistants for two years in the Department of Sociology at UCLA. Arlene Dallalfar contributed to Chapter 6 and prepared the list of specialized reference sources for sociology.

Lisa Frohmann received her M.A. in sociology from UCLA where she is a Ph.D. candidate. She has been an instructor and teaching assistant in sociology of sex roles, deviance, and mental illness, and in communication studies. Lisa Frohmann contributed major portions to Chapter 7 and had primary responsibility for the index.

Roseann Giarrusso holds an M.A. in sociology from UCLA, where she is currently completing her Ph.D., and also has an M.A. in psychology. As an instructor and teaching associate, she has taught a variety of courses in both fields, and has conducted workshops on how to succeed in college through skills development. She has also worked on a variety of research projects and has presented papers at professional conferences in sociology and psychology. Roseann Giarrusso contributed major portions to Chapters 2 and 3; Chapter 9 is her work.

Nancy A. Matthews has an M.A. in sociology from UCLA where she is a Ph.D. candidate. She has assisted in teaching political sociology, American society, and sociology of the family and has taught courses in introduction to sociology, race relations, and sociology of women. Nancy A. Matthews prepared the introductions to the sample papers and the Introduction to Part II. She also contributed to Chapters 1 and 7.

Judith Richlin-Klonsky holds an M.A. in sociology from UCLA where she is a Ph.D. candidate, and has an M.A. in marriage and family therapy. As a teaching assistant, she has worked with undergraduates in a variety of courses, including social control, the sociology of mental illness, medical sociology, and introductory sociology. Judith Richlin-Klonsky contributed major portions of Chapters 1, 4, 6, and 7. Chapter 8 is her work.

William G. Roy received his Ph.D. from the University of Michigan and is an associate professor of sociology at UCLA. He has published in major sociological journals on political sociology and historical sociology. William G. Roy wrote the "Framing a Question" and "Logic and Structure" sections of Chapter 1 and contributed to the development of the chapter as a whole.

Ellen Strenski received her Ph.D. from the University of Reading, England, and is a lecturer in UCLA Writing Programs where she coordinates writing across the curriculum. She has designed and taught writing courses attached to a variety of academic disciplines, including sociology. In addition to co-authoring *The Research Paper Workbook* (New York: Longman, 2d. ed., 1985) and *Making Connections Across the Curriculum: Readings for Analysis* (Boston: Bedford Books, 1986), she has published in many pedagogical journals on the subject of writing in diverse disciplines. Ellen Strenski contributed major portions to Chapters 5 and 6, and contributed to Chapter 7.

INDEX